# INTERIOR FINISHES

## FOR YOUR HOME

A J.B.Fairfax Press Publication

EDITORIAL
Craft Editor: Tonia Todman
Managing Editor: Judy Poulos
Editorial Coordinator: Margaret Kelly
Craft Assistants: Martina Oprey, Susie
Ting, Sally Pereira, Rosa Alonso

DESIGN AND PRODUCTION
Managers: Sheridan Carter, Nadia Sbisa
Layout: Tara Barrett, Julia Becker,
Gavin Murrell
Finished Art: Chris Hatcher,
Steven Joseph
Illustrations: Margie Mulray, Greg Gaul,
Carol Dunn, Rod Westblade
Photography: Harm Mol, Andrew Payne

Published by J.B. Fairfax Press Pty Ltd
80-82 McLachlan Avenue
Rushcutters Bay NSW Australia 2011
Ph: (02) 361 6366 Fax: (02) 360 6262

A.C.N. 003 738 430

INTERIOR FINISHES FOR YOUR HOME
ISBN 1 86343 110 1

Formatted by J.B. Fairfax Press Pty Ltd
Output by Adtype, Sydney
Printed by Toppan Printing Co, Hong Kong

# Contents

Laura Ashley (Australia) Pty Limited

# the first Steps

*The secret of successful home decorating is to combine careful planning and a sensible budget with your own creative flair and energy. If you research the project thoroughly, you'll wind up having a lot of fun, learn skills, save money **and** increase the value of your home. On top of all that, there's the satisfaction of knowing you did it yourself.*

## What are your needs?

❏ Is this your first nest? Does it look a bit tired and in need of some tender loving care?

❏ Have you lived there for many years? Do you feel it's time for a change now that the children are nearly off your hands and you can indulge your own tastes at long last?

❏ Are you renting an apartment, and limited in the amount of redecoration you can attempt, but want to update with new curtains and bright accessories?

A business couple who spend little time in their tiny city apartment have different needs to young parents with two children and a dog. Students need more bookshelves and study space than a single parent with a couple of active toddlers in tow.

Have a good look at what you can live with for a little bit longer and what just has to go right now. Fake it, if you can, with budget-conscious decorative

paint techniques for walls, floors and furniture (see pages 32-49).

A good scrub with sugar soap works wonders on tired walls and ceilings. It could enable you to postpone a full paint job in the bathroom, allowing you to spend a little more on new curtains or a beautifully framed print for the living room.

Make sure your planned renovations are user-friendly and will actually improve your quality of life. If you want to start a family next year, don't choose a plush upholstery fabric – it simply isn't practical.

If you are an apartment dweller or rent your home, consider the advantages of portable decorating projects, such as cushions, loose covers and accessories. Wonderful effects can be achieved with a little ingenuity – and you can take them with you when you move!

Sit down with the family and discuss everyone's needs. Write

them down in a sturdy notebook – used wisely, this will become your 'bible' and you'll carry it everywhere. Add a pen, a good tape measure and a colour card and you are ready to begin exploring the possibilities. A camera for taking pictures from different angles in the home may prove useful.

## What can you afford?

Working to a budget is vital. Obviously you will have certain financial commitments that must take priority over new curtains or a pot of paint. Even if your decorating project won't cost much, decide how much you can afford and then stick to your budget! Decide how much cash you can spare now and, say, over the next year...or will you need to borrow money – and from whom? How does borrowing fit into your long term plans for holidays, new clothes, the children's education? Interest on borrowings can be a trap. That new chair you buy in the sale won't be a bargain if you buy it on credit and pay interest.

❏ Always ask if you can get a price reduction for cash, and shop around for the best price

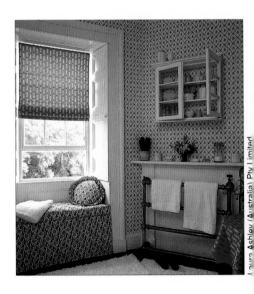

and service. Comparison shopping may take a little time but can save you lots of money. Take advantage of genuine sales, always buy the best product and most comprehensive service you can afford and do it right! A good carpet laid over a quality underlay is a better buy than a 'bargain' that doesn't wear well. You may have to wait a little longer for something special or do the work in stages, but it's worth the trouble to get what you really want. In the meantime, we can show you how to make beautiful alternatives that won't break the bank.

# Make your plans

A plan will help you to save money, avoiding those impulse buys (that you may regret the next day), and feel satisfied with the end results. After all, you'll have to live with them – perhaps for a long time.

This is when you really need your 'bible'.
❏ Measure everything – walls to estimate paint quantities, wallpaper and friezes; windows for tracks, rods and curtain fabric; floors for carpets and tiles; doors for new handles; furniture and cupboards…the lot!
❏ Take photographs of rooms and features you want to change.
❏ Making a floor plan is essential and it's easy if you use graph paper to scale down room sizes. Don't forget to include windows

and doors, steps, built-in cupboards, electrical and plumbing fittings room by room. Now you can cut out paper models of all your existing furniture to move around the paper plan, instead of dragging heavy furniture around the room.

Store the measurements, photographs and room plan in envelopes pasted inside the cover of your 'bible' so that you'll have them with you all the time. If you know the floor size of all your rooms, you'll be able to snap up a bargain when you see a carpet or tile sale.

# Calling in a professional

Paying a professional tradesman is unavoidable in some cases. Local regulations may demand that electrical, plumbing or building work is carried out by accredited tradespeople who

have the training, the tools and the authority to tackle some jobs which amateurs should never attempt. Check with your local authority.

# Get it in writing

This is the golden rule whenever you commission work. A written quote should include all costs and details of all materials to be used (quality and quantity); it should stipulate a completion date and must be written in clear language. Don't accept the quote unless you can understand it and accept everything in it. Ask for proof of the contractor's licence, or other accreditation. Check that you are adequately protected by his or her insurance, covering damage to your property and injury to anyone employed by the contractor to do your job.

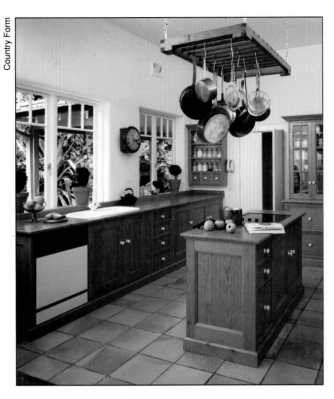

*Left: Natural timbers are the perfect choice for your kitchen. Properly prepared and sealed, they are easy to care for and pleasant to live with for many years*
*Below right: Putting together a new decorating scheme can be a great challenge and lots of fun! For a bright contemporary look, use lots of high tech, shiny chrome and strong colours*

## Do you need an interior designer?

Paying for advice from an interior designer is a sound investment if you can afford it. It costs nothing to ask for an 'advisory price' and scale of fees. Don't be embarrassed to say you have a budget – reputable designers will be delighted to find a client who knows how much he or she wants to spend. If you're not sure how to find a designer, refer to the local telephone directory. There may be a national association, such as The Interior Decorators' and Designers' Association, who will supply a list of their members. Or try chatting to staff at your favourite soft furnishing supplier. Some department stores offer a 'free' decorating service to their customers. There is no charge if you subsequently place an order, otherwise a nominal fee applies. To avoid misunderstandings and unexpected costs, ask for details before committing yourself.

## Plan your schedule

Good timing can help things run smoothly and can ease the financial burden of the work. Before you commission tradespeople to work for you, coordinate the job to be done – each stage has to be completed in the right sequence or you may face a lot of extra costs and many frustrating delays.

It's very important to allow sufficient time to do a good job – don't try to rush it. If you can't quite afford the exact curtains you want, maybe you could manage with lining fabric for a while? If you think the job is too big to tackle on your own, organise a 'working bee'. You supply the materials and all the food and drinks (and the work!) and ask family and friends to come over and lend a hand in return for a few laughs and refreshments.

Learning can be fun, whether you're acquiring new skills or brushing up old ones. We'll help you with tips on choosing fabric and displaying your accessories,

and we'll show you clever ways with paint and paper. You can also take classes in colour, lighting, painting techniques, tile-laying. You name it, somebody's teaching it! Take a course in household repairs and restoration – a sound investment which will teach you how to save money by doing your own repairs. Remember, knowing the 'nuts and bolts' of a job helps you tell the difference between a fair quote and a rip-off.

## Decorating with colour

Choosing the right colour is as important when decorating your house as it is when choosing your clothes – you live in both of them! Colour is affected by lighting (particularly artificial lights) and where you use it. You can make rooms seem bigger, smaller, taller, wider, or even create a special mood, with the right colours.

Whenever you select furnishings or paint, take a sample home so that you can judge the colour in the place and lighting conditions you have planned for it.

## Collecting samples

Collecting samples will become a passion once you start planning. Fabric swatches, scraps of wallpaper and friezes, paint cards, colour wheels and lighting brochures will burst from your 'bible'. Your diary will be filled with appointments to view

carpets, curtains, blinds and furnishings at home (check that this service is obligation-free). Seeing them at home is the most efficient way to choose colours and textures for large areas – and cuts your time and fuel costs, too!

## Trial and error

Before starting a big project, try out your ideas on a small scale. Buy sample-sized pots of paint and try them on the wall, remembering that colours can change. For instance, pastels paint up three or four times more intensely than they appear on a colour card.

All laminated surfaces can be painted – the trick is to find the right 'key' or surface preparation to accept the paint. Treat a small, unobtrusive section first to test your 'key' before embarking on the entire job.

Don't be deterred by little disappointments and mistakes. They're all learning experiences that can help you avoid costly problems when you tackle the real thing. Keep a record of tests and results, successes and failures in your 'bible' for future reference. Note what went wrong and if you were able to correct it – a photograph might help, too. Living with your new look is the best part. Looking at a beautiful finish and knowing you did it yourself is a very satisfying experience.

Now you have an endless source of suggestions for fellow do-it-yourself fans and, if you were clever enough to take 'before' and 'after' photos for your 'bible', you will have the best brag book in town!

So off you go – just remember

the basic principles of good planning, sensible budgeting and learning from your mistakes. When you've finished the first project, start another one. We have lots of suggestions for you and practical, easy to follow instructions. Good luck!

# Windows
## *with style*

*B*righten a dull room in a flash
with new curtains or practical,
sophisticated fabric blinds. Decide
which look best suits your window,
the rest of your decor and lifestyle.
If you like the softness of gathered
and ruffled material, combined with
the decorating possibilities of today's
wonderful fabric prints, then curtains
are more your style. If you prefer the
clean lines and monochromatic feel
of the city apartment, then Roman
blinds are just right for you.

# Simple Curtains

*Making your own curtains is not at all difficult and very economical.*

## Before You Begin

❏ You will need to measure the window you wish to cover with curtains.

❏ To calculate your length, measure from the top of the curtain track to the floor or window-sill or, in the case of a curtain pole and rings, measure from the eye hook at the bottom of the rings to the floor. Allow an extra 20 cm in total for turning under at the top and bottom. Curtains will finish approximately 5 cm above the top of the track or eye hook of the ring.

❏ The width measurement will depend on the thickness of your fabric. For very sheer fabrics you will need up to 3 times the length of the curtain track. For medium-weight fabrics you will need $2^1/2$ times the length of the track while twice the track length is acceptable for heavier fabrics.

❏ Sheer fabrics are traditionally not lined. Medium-weight fabrics can benefit from lining, as lined curtains become good insulators and are most effective in controlling light. Try to make your curtain linings the same colour on all your windows, otherwise the exterior view could become a patchwork of multi-coloured linings. You will need the same width of lining as for your main fabric. Lining fabrics are often very wide, so you may need to buy less fabric than for your main fabric.

❏ Consult your curtain accessory shop about the most appropriate heading tape for your fabric. Which one you choose will depend on the type of track or pole you have installed, the weight of your fabric and the effect you want – normally standard gathered tape, pencil pleat or triple pleat (also called pinch pleat). Our curtains have a thick wooden rod over which wooden rings are threaded. These have a small ring at the bottom through which the heading tape hook is inserted. You will need a length of heading tape equal to the total width of your curtain plus 10 cm for side hems and ease. For example, if you use four drops of 115 cm wide fabric will need 4.70 m of tape.

*Top: The fabric-covered pole and painted-to-match curtain rings*
*Above: The back of the curtain showing the pleating tape and the way in which it is pleated using the special hooks available where you buy the tape*
*Above right: The simple curtain with pleated heading, fabric-covered curtain pole and fittings painted to match the fabric*

### MATERIALS

☐ sufficient main fabric for curtain (see *Before You Begin*)
☐ sufficient lining fabric (see *Before You Begin*)
☐ sufficient heading tape (see *Before You Begin*)
☐ sufficient rings or hooks for your track or pole
☐ matching sewing threads

### METHOD

See the Pull Out Pattern Sheet at the back of the book for the window measurement diagram.

**1** Cut your main fabric and lining into the lengths you have calculated in *Before You Begin*.

**2** Stitch main fabric lengths together down the long sides until you have the complete curtain width. Do this for lining lengths as well. Turn under 1 cm on the outside edges of main fabric piece then turn under another 5 cm. Baste. Stitch along inner fold. Do this for lining piece as well, folding under 7 cm at sides.

**3** Press both pieces. Place them together with wrong sides facing so that 1 cm of main fabric extends beyond the lining on both sides, and top and bottom raw edges are even. Turn over 3 cm of both curtain and lining *together* at top. Press and pin in place.

**4** If using pencil pleating tape, unravel the draw cords of the first 5 cm of the tape. For triple pleating tape, such as

**6** Turn up curtain hem. Pin and baste. Turn up the lining hem to sit 2 cm shorter than the curtain. Remove the curtain from the track. Stitch both hems. Press to finish.

## Fabric-covered pole

### MATERIALS
- ☐ wooden curtain pole
- ☐ sufficient wooden curtain rings
- ☐ a pair of finials (end stoppers)
- ☐ sufficient fabric to cover (see *Before You Begin*)
- ☐ fabric or craft glue

### METHOD

**1** Cut a rectangular piece of fabric the length of the pole and the width of the circumference of the pole plus 3 cm for overlap.

**2** If not using the selvage of the fabric, finish one long edge of the fabric by folding under 6 mm. Wrap the fabric around the pole with the folded edge covering the raw edge. Glue into place.

**3** Finials can also be covered by using fabric cut on the bias, pleating out the fullness and cutting out these small pleats so that fabric lies flat with no gaps. The pattern will not match on these pieces, but it does not seem to matter! If you are worried by the possibility of gaps, you can paint the finials the same colour as the background colour of the fabric before you begin covering the pole.

**4** You can cover all the rings with fabric too. Or you can simply paint them in a colour to complement your fabric.

*Below: Sometimes all you need is a little imagination! You can make this elegant, draped pelmet simply by trimming a suitable length of fabric and draping it over your curtain track or pole as shown here. Take care that the right side of your fabric is always the one showing*

ours, turn in raw end of tape so that you have a hook channel just in from the edge of the curtain. Pin the upper edge of the tape to the curtain 1.5 cm down from the top. Stitch down all edges of the tape. If you are using pencil pleating tape, draw up the cords to gather the curtain and insert the hooks into the channels. If you are using triple pleating tape, insert the pronged hooks according to the manufacturer's instructions. This will give the pleated effect.

**5** Hang the curtain and leave it to hang for twenty-four hours to allow the fabric to ease and 'drop'. After twenty-four hours, and while the curtains are still hanging, make the connecting 'ties' between the side edges of the curtain and lining .

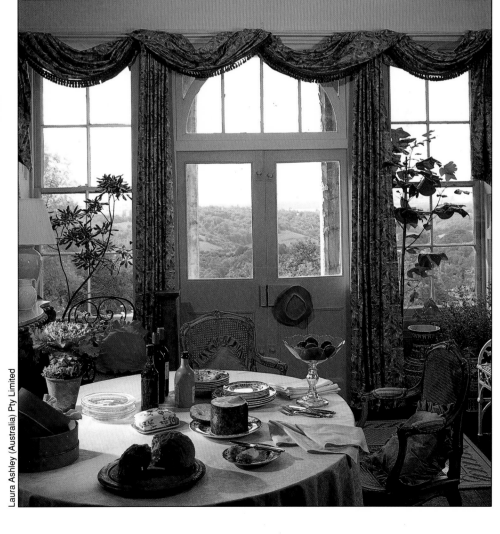

Laura Ashley (Australia) Pty Limited

# *Down to* DETAIL

## Café Curtains

*This simple method of window dressing will afford privacy and at the same time allow plenty of light to enter the room. Café curtains can be casual or formal, soft and feminine or dramatically contemporary, depending on the fabric you choose. Plain fabrics can be stencilled, appliquéd or braid-trimmed.*

### Before You Begin

❑ Proportion is important when making café curtains. Generally, the lower curtains are at least half the length of the window and look best when they are approximately five-eighths of the length. The length of the upper curtain should complement that of the lower one but still allow a gap to let in light. It is usually one-quarter of the length of the window, or a little less.

❑ These curtains do not use stitch-on pleating tape, rather they rely on casings in the upper curtain and self fabric loops for the lower curtains which allow for insertion of the rods. The lower curtains are two identical curtains which part in the middle.

❏ Remember to measure from the top of the rods when calculating fabric lengths for both curtains. Add a hem and casing allowance to each fabric drop (i.e. length of fabric) – 20 cm for the upper curtain and 26 cm for the lower curtain. For example, assuming that your upper curtain is to finish 30 cm from the top of the rod and your lower curtain is to finish 50 cm from the top of the lower rod, you will need to cut your upper curtain into drops of 50 cm, and your lower curtain into drops of 76 cm.

❏ Generally, you will find each curtain requires a total fabric width of 2¼ times the length of the rod. If you are using a sheer fabric, or lace, you may wish to increase this to 2½ times or even 3 times the length of the rod. For example, if your rod is 1 m long, you will need to seam together enough fabric drops to produce a total width of 2.25 m plus side and centre turn under allowances.

❏ To calculate fabric quantities for our curtains on your window follow the simple formulas below.
*For the upper curtain* the total length of the drops required to make up the required width, allowing 10 cm in total for side hems plus 20 cm per drop for casing and hem.
*For the lower curtain* the total length of the drops required to make up the required width, allowing 20 cm in total for side and centre hems plus 26 cm per drop for casing loops and hem.

## MATERIALS
☐ sufficient fabric for upper and lower curtains (see *Before You Begin*)
☐ matching sewing thread
☐ strong handsewing needle
☐ curtain pole, brackets and rings

## METHOD
**For the upper curtain:**
1 Join short ends of fabric drops to create the total width. Turn in 1 cm on the side edges, then turn another 4 cm and press. Stitch along the inner fold.

2 Turn over 1 cm on upper edge, then turn another 8 cm and press. Stitch along the inner fold. Stitch again 4 cm from previous stitching, creating the rod casing. The fabric above the casing will form a frill when the rod is inserted.

3 Turn up 1 cm on the lower edge, then turn another 4 cm and press. Stitch along the first fold. Press.

**For the lower curtains:**
See the Pull Out Pattern Sheet at the back of the book for the template for the cut out.

1 The instructions are for one curtain. Make two the same. Join fabric drops, if necessary, to create the required width for the lower curtain. Turn in 1 cm on one side of curtain, then turn another 4 cm and press. Stitch along the first fold.

2 Fold 1 cm over to the wrong side on the top edge and press. Fold over another 25 cm on the top edge so that right sides are facing. Press.

3 Cut a cardboard template from the shape on the pattern sheet. Check that this is long enough to loop over your curtain pole, and adjust its size if necessary. Place the template at the top edge, 8 cm in from the hemmed side edge of the curtain. Mark the shapes across the curtain, about 10 cm apart or to suit your fabric pattern. Mark where you will place the final scallop, leaving 8 cm as on the other end and allowing for the side hem. Cut off any excess fabric.

4 Open out the marked top of the curtain. Turn in 1 cm along the side edge, then turn another 4 cm and press. Stitch along first crease. Fold the top of the curtain again. Stitch around the marked shapes and cut out. Trim and clip into curves for ease. Turn loops to the right side and press. At the back, bring the top of the loop to the base of the loop. Stitch through all thicknesses.

5 Thread the pole through the loops to hang the curtain.

6 If you wish to cover the curtain pole with matching fabric, this is quite easy to do. You can use your curtain fabric or you can choose a contrasting one. See the instructions on page 11 for how to cover your curtain pole.

*Top left: The upper curtain showing the rod casing and frill*
*Centre left: The lower curtain showing the rod threaded through the loops*

# Festoon or Cloud Blinds

*For a romantic look, nothing beats festoon blinds. The fabric you choose will set the style for your blind, from the soft and feminine look of sheer lace to the dramatic elegance of silk brocade. These are in simple homespun cotton for a contemporary feel.*

## Before You Begin

❏ To calculate your fabric requirements, measure the width and length of your window. You will need a piece of fabric twice this length by twice this width. If you need to join fabric to achieve this width, do so with small flat seams.

MATERIALS

**For each blind:**
- ☐ fabric (see *Before You Begin*)
- ☐ pencil pleating tape, twice the width of your window
- ☐ ring tape, four times your blind length plus 24 cm
- ☐ one cleat for fastening blind cords
- ☐ metal rod or dowelling for holding lower

edge, 1 cm in diameter to measure 2.5 cm shorter than the width of the window.
- ☐ eyelet screws – one for each length of ring tape plus one
- ☐ curtain track of your choice
- ☐ sufficient hooks for fastening blind to track

METHOD

See the Pull Out Pattern Sheet at the back of the book for the cord threading diagram.

1 Turn in 2.5 cm on the top and sides of fabric piece (or joined pieces). Press.

2 Unravel the draw cords of the first 5 cm of the pencil pleating tape. Pin the upper edge of the tape to the top of your blind fabric, 1.5 cm from the edge. Stitch down all edges of the tape, stitching the top hem as you go. Do not draw up the cords.

3 Turn under 1 cm on the lower edge and then turn another 4 cm. Press. Stitch bottom hem.

4 Stitch ring tape down side hems (fixing hems in place at the same time), and at two equally-spaced points across the blind from top to bottom hems. Leave an extra 6 cm of tape at the bottom of each length.

5 Loop this tape back on itself so that the end is just above the hem. Stitch. These loops are to hold the bottom rod.

6 Gather pencil pleating cord, until the blind gathers to the width of the track.

7 Attach eyelets to the window frame, just below the track, to correspond with the top of each strip of ring tape and another, just below one curtain track bracket, through which you will thread blind cords.

8 Cut a cord for each strip of tape, long enough to reach from the bottom rod, up the blind, through the eyelets, across the top and down to the side where the extra eyelet is, leaving sufficient length for knotting them together below the eyelet.

9 Thread the cords up from the bottom, tying the three bottom rings together as you go to form a permanent blousing effect. Attach the blind to the curtain track with the hooks. Insert the rod through the tape loops at the lower edge of the blind.

# Roman Blinds

*For a more tailored window treatment, consider these Roman blinds.*

## Before You Begin

❏ Roman blinds are traditionally fitted inside the window frame. They retain one or two pleats even when let down. Take this into account when measuring.

❏ To calculate your fabric requirements: You will need the desired width of the blind plus 10 cm for hems x the desired length of the blind plus 30 cm at the top for turning plus 12 cm for each timber lath plus 13 cm for the lower hem and lath pocket.

❏ Decide how many lath pockets you want to have by making a paper pattern of the blind. Fold in the 30 cm at the top and the 5 cm at the lower edge and then crease in the lath pockets. Do this until you are happy with the number and spacing of your laths – generally six or eight.

❏ Fabrics with strong patterns or ones that do not adequately screen the light, may need to be lined. Cut the lining fabric the same size as the main fabric. Baste the two pieces together, with wrong sides facing, and from here on treat them as a single layer, following the instructions below. Remember to choose a lining fabric in keeping with that on the other windows so your house is as attractive from the outside as it is inside.

## MATERIALS

❏ sufficient fabric and lining (optional) (see *Before You Begin*)
❏ 5 cm wide contrast fabric strip or braid x four times the length of the blind, before stitching the pockets
❏ matching sewing thread
❏ sufficient 5 cm wide timber laths, as wide as the finished width of the blind (see *Before You Begin*)
❏ a mounting board the width of your window, 2 cm thick and 7 cm deep.
❏ one pair metal 'L' brackets
❏ tacks or a staple gun
❏ nylon cord about 6 mm thick for raising and lowering the blind
❏ sufficient eye hooks to have two for

each lath, two on the mounting board and one more at one end of the mounting board
❏ one metal cleat for tying off the cords

## METHOD

See the Pull Out Pattern Sheet at the back of the book for the construction diagram.

**1** Turn 1 cm on both sides of the blind fabric piece to the right side. Press. Turn in 1 cm on long sides of contrast fabric strips. Press. Pin one strip to each edge of the blind, covering the pressed raw edge and having the pressed edges of the strip and blind matching. Stitch both long edges of the contrast strip to the blind. Stitch the other two strips one-third of the way in from the sides. Turn 1 cm on the upper and lower edges to the wrong side. Press. On the lower edge turn under 6 cm and stitch down, forming the last lath pocket.

**2** Mark each lath pocket with two lines 12 cm apart. On the outside of the fabric, bring these two lines together. Pin and baste along marked lines. Stitch, forming the lath pockets. Carefully stitch the folded edge of each lath pocket down onto the blind. Insert the laths.

**3** On the wrong side of the blind, screw an eye hook through the fabric into each lath about a quarter of the way in from the sides. Make sure that all your hooks run down the blind in a straight line.

**4** Attach your mounting board to the wall above the window frame with metal 'L' brackets.

**5** Tack or staple the top edge of the fabric to the top of the mounting board, close to the back (wall) edge so that the fabric covers the top of the board and hangs down the front of it, concealing the board altogether. Screw two eye hooks into the underside of the mounting board, each one in line with a row of eye hooks on the blind. Screw another eye hook into one end of the underside of the mounting board on the same side as you will mount the cleat for holding the cords on the window frame.

**6** Secure a cord at the lowest eye hook on each side of the blind. Thread the cords up the row of eye hooks on the blind, including those on the mounting board, so that both cords emerge at the extra eye hook on one side of the mounting board. Knot the cords together below the level of the cleat.

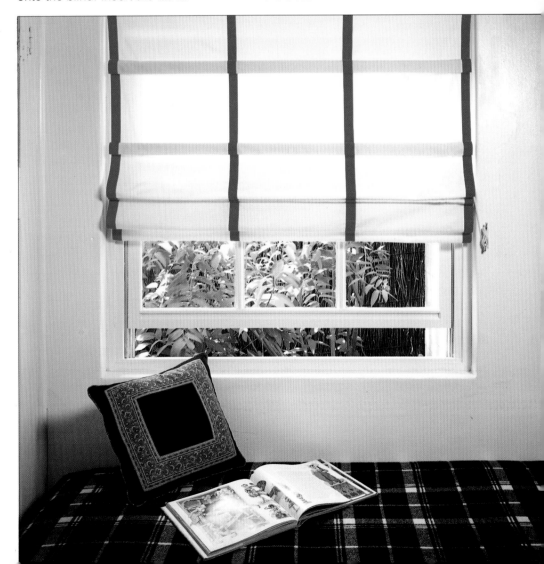

# *Down to* DETAIL

## Leadlight Porthole

*There is nothing quite like a well-designed and well-made leadlight window. Pinpoints of light and flashes of colour can transform a boring window with a poor view into a major feature. Leadlighting is perhaps one of those projects that should not be undertaken as a one-off project.*

### MATERIALS

- [ ] 15 mm 'H' section round lead cames for edges
- [ ] 4.2 mm, 5.2 mm and 5.5 mm 'H' section round lead cames for centre
- [ ] selected glass – in this case, German machine antique glass
- [ ] 50:50 solder stick
- [ ] horseshoe nails
- [ ] flux
- [ ] leadlighting putty
- [ ] whiting
- [ ] stove black

### SPECIAL TOOLS NEEDED

Leadlighting requires specialised equipment. Making your existing tools do the job will not produce the best results. The tools are generally only available from stained glass materials suppliers.

- [ ] ordinary steel wheel cutter
- [ ] good quality tungsten carbide glass cutter, if using selenium oxide glass. If not self lubricating, organise a small container to hold the lubricant – a mixture of light oil and kerosene
- [ ] glass pliers
- [ ] cut running pliers
- [ ] grozing pliers
- [ ] electric soldering iron, 80 watt with 'hook nose' tip
- [ ] lead vice and pliers
- [ ] lathekin
- [ ] lead knife, such as Don Carlos pattern
- [ ] wire brush

### METHOD

**Note:** Washing hands thoroughly after working with lead should be automatic, as lead is an accumulative poison.

1 Set up an area to work on that is flat and will not damage the glass. A workbench with a particle/chip board top is ideal. A felt covering will protect the glass from scratching. As work progresses the surface should be vacuumed of glass splinters frequently as these may damage or break the glass being cut.

2 Finalise your design. This is often the slowest part of the job, but many books on the subject have a number of designs that can be used or adapted. Try to avoid designs where tight curves

*Right: An entrance showing a door with leadlight panels and a leadlight porthole*
*Below: Interior view of leadlight porthole*

or sharp internal corners need to be cut, because you probably won't be successful. Plain shapes with relatively simple curves are easiest to cut and lead up.

3 Once the design is drawn, make several copies and colour them in with the colours you've selected. It may be worthwhile trying several combinations of colours to get it just right.

4 Measure the window. In this case, it is a 415 mm circular window. Deduct half the width of the lead (came), in this case about 7 mm, plus an additional 3 mm from the circle all round to allow for fitting. Large 'H' section lead is used on edges to allow for trimming should the pattern 'grow' slightly while being made. Therefore the pattern (cartoon) size is finalised at 400 mm in diameter.

5 Transfer your design to the full pattern size and make a full-scale drawing of the window. Do it in pencil first to ensure it is right. Then finally draw it in heavy felt pen to leave a line about 1.5 mm thick between the glass pieces. This automatically makes an allowance for the wall thickness of the lead section.

6 Make a couple of copies of the pattern, so that they can be used for numbering glass pieces, or cut into individual pieces and used as templates for cutting the glass (if you find that easiest), or if one gets damaged or torn.

7 Mount your main cartoon on a piece of particle/chip board or something similar, with plenty of room to work around the edges of the design. Normally, two battens are fixed to the board against which you can work. In the case of this circular design, mark out and cut a panel to fit against the battens, then mark out and cut a semicircle to hold the lead in place. In this example, glass was used as the panel, but you can use thin plywood.

8 Choose the coloured glass for each shape according to your design; buy it and have it ready to start. Similarly, have the lead ready, as well as horseshoe nails and all other needs.

9 Cut the first piece of glass to size. This should be a piece of scrap just for practice. Start the cut a small distance in from the edge of the glass. Apply steady pressure without stopping, and hold the cutter close to 90°. Draw it towards you,

*Left: Drawing of the porthole, showing different colour sections*
*Below: Template of the leadlight porthole*

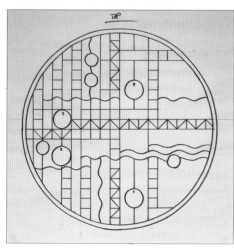

**16** Cut off the two damaged ends of the lead, and then cut sufficient length off the wider lead to place around the semicircle defined by the cut panel. The lead is cut using a sharp lead knife, in a rocking motion. The other half of the perimeter is the last piece in the jigsaw to be fitted at the end.

**17** Select the piece of glass for the starting point. On our circle it can just about be anywhere on the bottom perimeter, but where successive pieces can be installed easily. The best place would be in the middle. This particular window was made by building up from the bottom, filling in all the lower area and then working up the centre and out to the sides.

**18** Insert the first piece of glass, gently tapping it into place with the wooden end of the lead knife. Hold it in place with horseshoe nails, with the flat side of the nails against the glass.

**19** Cut a length of the internal (thinner) lead slightly longer than the edge to be joined, and insert the adjoining glass into the lead. Hold it in place using the horseshoe nails. Mark the joint of the two glass pieces on the lead, taking care to get the angle right, and remove the lead. Make another mark just back from this first one, and cut the lead slightly short. This allows for the next lead, which crosses the first one, to sit properly with an accurate joint that will be easy to solder. Slowly continue in this fashion, fanning out across the window, building up the leadlight. Always hold each new piece or section with the horseshoe nails. Never use the nails against the lead as they will cause irreparable damage because of the softness of the lead.

**20** When the entire leadlight has been made, the final outside wider came is fitted in place and you are ready to solder the joints. At this point, measure the panel for size.

**21** Just before soldering, ensure that no flanges from the lead are bent onto the glass or out of shape, because once soldered, they will be set.

**22** Soldering is done with an 80 watt iron, as this heats up quickly. Lower wattage irons can be used, but may be a little slower. The easiest tip to use is a 'hook nose' tip, or angled tip as pictured

---

and let it roll over the edge near you.

**10** To break the glass, hold it vertically and place your two index fingers under either side of the cut, and your thumbs on top of the glass – the knuckles should be touching. Rotate both hands down, or clockwise and anticlockwise, and the glass should break and 'run' along your score line. Shake off any splinters.

If the glass will not break, lightly tap under the score line with the hammer on the non-cutting end of the glass cutter. Hold the glass close to the score line to avoid breakage.

**11** If you are still unsuccessful using your fingers, you may have to invest in a pair of cut running pliers to do the job. When cutting thin strips it may be necessary to use grozing pliers to grip the

narrow side, or you may injure your hand if you slip. Glass cut in this way will never be as neat as when it is cut by running.

**12** When cutting the glass for actual leadlight, mark out from the cartoon directly, or the cut-out pieces. Cut the large pieces first as the offcuts may then be used for smaller pieces of the same colour. Aim at being economical – within reason.

**13** Once it has been cut, hold each piece against your pattern and make sure it fits between the inked-in lines. If it overlaps it will need trimming with the grozing pliers. If it is too small it will need to be recut.

**14** Generally leadlighters like to cut all the glass pieces to shape before starting the leading. The pieces can be laid on the spare cartoon, or each piece can be numbered on the face side with a corresponding number on the spare cartoon. The pieces can be carefully laid in a box until ready for use.

**15** Before lead can be used, it must be stretched, and this is done with a lead vice and pliers. This must be done with care so that when you apply pressure, the lead does not snap, dumping you on the floor. Once stretched, the channels of the lead may need to be opened using a lathekin. You may be able to purchase prestretched lead.

below. The tip should be properly tinned before use. Soldering must be carried out in the presence of flux, which removes oxide from the surface of the lead and provides a good surface for the solder to adhere to. Solid flux is recommended because it is easiest to clean up afterwards. Rub the flux over the joint to be soldered.

**23** Start soldering at the point furthest away from where you are standing. Hold the iron close to the lead and take a small blob of solder from the stick. Place this on the joint. It should run on to the joint and, when the iron is removed, will soon set. Use a little at a time; you can always add more if the joint looks scantly soldered.

**24** When all the joints are soldered, take a wire brush and brush off all traces of flux on the window. Any solder spilt on the glass or lead should be peeled off as well.

**25** Turn the window over together with the base as the window is still not strong. Repeat the soldering on the back side. Once again, remove the leftover flux.

**26** It's now time to putty the window. This must be done in one sitting, otherwise it will set and leave oil stains. Use prepared leadlighting putty, which has been made with carbon black. Wear old clothes as this is a messy job. Force

the putty under the lead flanges with whatever you find easiest, thumbs or the lathekin. Do not press down too hard on the glass as the panels can break very easily. Excess putty can be removed by carefully scraping with the lathekin or by using a horse-shoe nail alongside the lead.

**27** At this stage, sprinkle whiting over the surface of the whole window and scrub vigorously to clean it. Don't press too hard, as the whole window is still a little soft and may distort. Repeat the process on the other side.

**28** Let the window stand, rather than lie, for a few days to allow the putty to harden. After three days or so, decide whether you would like a grey or a black finish. If grey, simply polish the window with a bristle brush. If you want the lead to be black, apply some well-mixed black with a brush. After a few minutes, when the solvent has

evaporated, polish with a brush once again. Never use a cloth as it tends to shine the soldered joints silver.

**29** Now install the window in the previously prepared frame.

*Top: Cutting glass for the leadlight porthole*
*Above: Assembling the glass pieces and lead*
*Right: Soldering the lead joints with a `hook nose' soldering iron*

# Tracks and Rods
## FEATURE

Your choice of curtain rods, poles or tracks will be based on the shape and function of your window, the effect you want to create – and your budget. If you live in rented accommodation, you should opt for rods or poles which are usually less expensive, easier to install and highly portable. Special extendable poles allow you to change the length to suit different windows – another plus for rent-payers!

Unless curtains are frequently drawn, poles are the answer for heavy drapes, framing a window, or lightweight privacy curtains. More sophisticated poles may be fitted with draw-cords, gliders and decorative finials (those pretty end-stops that stop the curtains from sliding off the pole). Prices will vary according to the style you choose.

Tracks range from simple, straight or curved styles to pricier, composite products which can support both curtains and a ruffled pelmet. These may have extension brackets to vary the distance between the curtains, walls and the pelmet.

If you are seeking a permanent arrangement, don't skimp on quality by using cheap, unreliable tracks. Remember to match hooks, gliders and end-stops to the style of curtain-heading tape

you have chosen. Pelmets hide a multitude of sins and save money because you can fit plainer tracks or rods than those required by exposed curtain heads.

Beautiful curtains must sit squarely on accurately positioned fittings. Arm yourself with a retractable fibreglass or metal tape measure and carefully measure window dimensions, frame size and the distance to the ceiling, floor and corners of adjacent walls. These measurements are essential when planning special effects, such as creating an impression of height on a shallow window. You can do this by hanging long curtains from poles or tracks raised well above the natural top of the window or even suspended from the ceiling.

Always anchor rods or tracks firmly with strong brackets, screwed to wooden battens or wall plugs. You will need to find out what's underneath your wall or ceiling plaster. If you arrange a free measure and quote from several reputable curtain makers (who will have to determine the construction materials to calculate costs), you'll be able to compare their prices and ask all your questions at no cost!

If you can avoid it, don't hang new curtains on old tracks or poles. Choose fittings appropriate to the shape and style of your curtains. Heavy curtains may require special reinforcement, especially if they will be frequently opened and closed. Purchased kits should contain everything you'll need to complete the job: poles or tracks, strong brackets, sufficient hooks and gliders, and screws long enough to anchor brackets. Very long poles and tracks may need extra supporting brackets spaced at intervals between the usual end and centre brackets.

Choose fittings that frame your windows beautifully and do their job. Heavy curtains should completely retract to maximise light. For recessed windows, select flexible or curved metal tracks to fit the shape of the modern bay windows, hung with one continuous curtain or three separate curtains. Traditional bay windows, in three sections separated by wide corner frames, can use a single track or three separate curtain poles.

Instead of end-stops or finials, fit the last hook to a wall-mounted ring-fitting to hide track ends and avoid ugly gaps between curtains and walls. Never hang curtains straight across the face of a recessed window: they darken the room and detract from the charm of a traditional bay or dormer window.

# Borders and Trims
## FEATURE

Introduce the personal touch to soft furnishings with wonderful braids and trims. Today's furnishings are increasingly ornate and generous in proportion. There is a pronounced trend towards softness and fullness in design, whether it's in the lines of well-padded sofas and soft feather-filled cushions or generous metres of fabric, draped across curtains to form swagged pelmets or gathered into festoon blinds.

Interior designers have always valued the extra 'something' given to a piece of furniture or accessory by the addition of well-chosen trims. Most stockists of furnishing fabrics have a good range of trims to choose from, and many are surprisingly inexpensive. While cost is a most important consideration, if only because it is possible to over-trim an inexpensive fabric, there are several other considerations to bear in mind when selecting your borders and trims.

Matching of styles is important. Common sense is the key here, and while creativity frequently challenges rules of colour and suitability, your 'eye' will tell you if a trim matches a fabric. Fabrics that are generally dull rather than lustrous tend to look casual – while shimmery fabrics will always have a more formal look. You need to look at trims in the same way. Simple rickrack braid will look smart but informal, and so too will bias binding, twill braids, checked

ribbons and cotton laces. Lustrous formal looks are enhanced by adding twisted silk cords and tassels, brocaded braids, metallic bindings and moiré taffeta and silk ribbons. Some decorators manage to achieve wonderful 'surprises' by the unusual marriage of trims and fabric. It takes considerable skill to pull this off successfully, so take care.

Too much of a contrasting trim will become the focal point. If this is not your intention, be conscious of the impact of the trim you are adding. This is not a problem if the trim is in the same colour as your fabric. In this case it will not compete with the fabric, rather it will add interesting textured effects.

Will the braid be as long-wearing as the fabric? Be mindful of where you use the trim; hand and headrests are more prone to wearing than the back of a sofa. It is sometimes a good idea to purchase more braid than you need right at the beginning to allow for replacement of worn areas.

Is the braid washable? Will the colour run in water? If you are planning to wash the trimmed item, you should wash the trim and the fabric first. This also applies if you are trimming an existing item . Sometimes a handful of household cooking salt thrown into cold rinsing water will help to 'set' dyes in trims, but it is always wise to be sure.

# Creating
## *a look*

*R*e-create your favourite decorating style at home with clever combinations of colour, texture and accessories. You may have to start with your existing rooms and furniture and ring the changes with our tips. Of course, if you are able to buy new furniture and fittings, it will certainly make your job a lot easier.

Country Form

IKEA

# Three Great Looks

## Classic

You can fake the elegant lines and smooth textures of the classic look by using single-colour themes and rich-looking synthetic fabrics. Oval coffee and side tables, polished timber cabinets and wall mirrors, reflecting floor-length curtains and swags,

*The Australian Wool Corporation*

*Dupont*

*Above: This elegant, classic living room shows the clever use of a subdued colour scheme and occasional furniture, lamps and ornaments to create the look*
*Left: The classic dining room features traditionally styled furniture, drapes and subtle lighting*

develop this formal style. Repeat curtain colour in synthetic taffeta lamp shades, piped cushions trimmed with small tassels, or in graceful accessories like Grandma's favourite vase, a soft floral painting or a beautiful piece of glass. Plan formal arrangements of old-fashioned roses, camellias, gladioli and iris or stand spathiphyllum, strelitzia, flowering cyclamen, begonia or anthuriums in highly polished brass or timber planters. Conceal clutter in cupboards and light the rooms with traditional table or standard lamps, recessed spot lights, pendants or wall sconces – but keep it simple.

## Contemporary

Simple lines and the smooth, cool textures of brushed or polished metals, glass, acrylic, polished timber and marble veneers reflect a no-fuss, contemporary approach. Upholstery options include leather or vinyl, linen or wool, lustrous satins or synthetics. The look is tailored and functional, without much fabric and absolutely no frills! Simple drapes and cushions in strong contrasting or neutral colours work with Roman and bonded blinds, slimline venetians or vertical drapes. Choose one or two accessories to develop the theme, such as an abstract poster or print or a slim ceramic vase. Strike a green note with a single kentia palm, yucca or pony tail plant in a streamlined container. Compose simple floral arrangements of stark foliage and one beautiful lily or strelitzia in simple glass, ceramic or terracotta containers. Abundant natural light is a feature of the contemporary look, augmented with track lighting and floor or table lamps on slim adjustable stands. Use geometric pendants or spotlights to highlight important features in a room. Stereo and video equipment, books and collectables stand on open shelving or in glass cabinets, but take care to conceal the clutter in cupboards.

26

# Country

Imitate the country folk who traditionally gather to make their own decorations with bright colours and lots of texture. Soften chunky pine or scrubbed timber furniture with tiny floral print fabrics or earthy homespuns, calico and wool. Treat used-furniture bargains with weathered paint techniques, or team rustic cane with frilly cushions. Select fabrics to complement existing colour schemes and add a touch of lace, a valance or handmade rag rug to achieve that country look. Accessorise with bright china plates hanging on walls; wreaths of dried grasses and seedpods framing small mirrors; toss a patchwork quilt on a sofa, bed or on a wall; hat and coat racks, watercolours and collections of almost anything from pebbles to milk jugs. Bunches of daisies, forget-me-nots or pansies and hanging baskets of ivy or maidenhair complement clustered pots of herbs, ferns and flowering geraniums or cineraria. Storage is open and cheerful. Have your shining pots stand on open dressers but camouflage modern appliances. Allow lots of natural light and, at night, turn on soft table lamps, cane-shaded pendants or electric 'oil' lamps.

*Right: This living room features the fabric, accessories and comfortable feel of the country style*
*Below: Natural timbers and stoneware accessories decorate this country kitchen*
*Below left: Simple lines and an absence of clutter are the marks of a contemporary room*

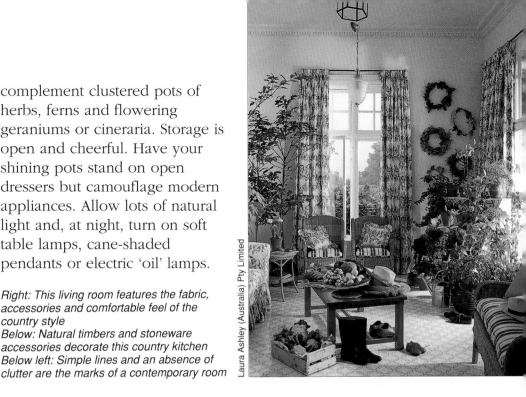

Laura Ashley (Australia) Pty Limited

Country Form

IKEA

# Personal Touche.

## FEATURE

Put the mark of your own personality into your decorating scheme. Your home, whether it's a big house or a rented room, should say something about you and your life.

The possibilities for adding that special, personal touch are as endless as your imagination. If you have a hobby, why not display you finished work, and even those pieces you are still working on, on table or dresser top. Sometimes a pleasing display of an assortment o objects that you enjoy looking at, makes a wonderful decorating and personal statement.

Don't be too worried about the tidiness of your display or even ho odd it may look. Be adventurous and you will be surprised at how much your visitors will enjoy looking at it and what a great ice-breaker it can be when entertaining

*Above: If you have odd pieces of unusual china that you've acquired over the years, don't hide it away in a cupboard but display it for everyone to admire*
*Right: An eclectic mixture of old Eastern brass, weights and measures and a delightful carved wooden shoe combined with the texture of an old water filter are sure conversation starters when displayed on this wooden mantle*
*Far right: A sunny corner blossoms with this arrangement of much loved bits and pieces and a lovely old bowl full of rosy onions*

*Above: Soften the hard look of a modern stairway with a display of old bottles, jars and even wheels*
*Above right: Dress up an open shelf with a handsome collection of rolling pins*
*Right: A few pieces of beautiful Chinese blue and white porcelain add the perfect finishing touch to any room*

# ways with Walls

*Walls need not be finished with plain paint any more. These days you have an almost endless variety of wallcoverings or wall finishes to choose from and they need not break the bank! You will find wallpapers for every room in your home from scrubbable vinyls for the kitchen to elegant flocked papers for your dining room and pretty florals for the bedroom. There are some surprisingly easy methods of using paint to create special effects, and the best news is that they will add only a little more to the initial cost of your paint. All you need is a lot of enthusiasm, a little energy and our easy-to-follow Down to Detail instructions for decorative painted finishes.*

# Down to DETAIL

## Paint Finishes

*The rough, cold cement floor of the living room, pictured opposite, now looks and feels like expensive inlaid stone blocks, costing nothing but your physical labour and a few tins of paint. Walls of a boring dark hall have been transformed into a gem-like Wedgwood box with the application of paint and some inexpensive plastic ornaments.*

A room, apparently panelled silk, is, in fact, painted to appear that way. Pale, subtle colour glows in soft dragged lines on surfaces which previously were flat and dead and of no interest. With your labour, some paint and a lot of enthusiasm, you can turn your home into a treasure house of colour, texture and warmth.

Special paint effects were once the province of skilled professional decorators – but not anymore! You can texture and colour your walls, woodwork and furniture in ways that will make them unique.

You can achieve broken colour finishes by using two very basic methods: a paint glaze is either added over a background colour with a sponge or by spattering; or the paint glaze is rolled or painted onto the background colour and then partially removed using rags, combs, stippling brushes and so on. Different tools produce quite different effects with the paint – and the way you manipulate each tool is all-important.

The colour and pattern you choose can add that magical – and often missing – element of style to a room's colour scheme.

They create wonderful illusions – the overall effect can look luxurious and very expensive, yet the process can be as cheap as the cost of the paint!

These finishes are suited to articles made from just about anything – wood, glass, ceramics, highly glazed pottery, leather and plastic.

Plastic items bought straight off the shelf from a supermarket or department store – a plastic jug, tray or wastepaper basket – can be very successfully transformed and stylised with a painted finish.

So many of the everyday objects that surround us can be completely re-created using painted finishes – old table mats, vases and tin canisters to name a few. Don't forget that these things all fit into your larger design and home colour scheme and can, in fact, add that essential 'just right' finishing touch.

*Below left: A stencilled kitchen wall*
*Below: A Wedgwood green hallway with trompe l'oeil door*
*Opposite: A living room with ragged and dragged walls and a stone-finished floor*
*Inset: A detail of the painted floor*

# Tools and Supplies

To achieve the best results, good tools and supplies are of the utmost importance. Buy them as you need them, beginning with the basics and adding to them as necessary.

- ❏ eggshell enamel (one part matt/flat enamel to one part satin enamel or one part matt/flat acrylic to one part satin acrylic)
- ❏ matt/flat enamel paints
- ❏ water-based artists' acrylics
- ❏ universal tints
- ❏ oil-based and water-based scumble medium
- ❏ turps (white spirit)
- ❏ shellac
- ❏ rollers
- ❏ methylated spirits
- ❏ roller covers
- ❏ roller pans (trays)
- ❏ wall stipple brush (rectangular)
- ❏ cutting-in (detail) brush, 50 mm
- ❏ 50 mm to 75 mm paint brushes
- ❏ dragging brush
- ❏ round stipple brush
- ❏ natural sponges
- ❏ calico (cut and washed) – buy new calico, cut in 20 m lengths, then wash it, put it through the dryer to remove lint, and cut it into short lengths
- ❏ containers for mixing
- ❏ large stirring sticks
- ❏ strainer bags (nylon tights)
- ❏ duster brush
- ❏ tack rags
- ❏ ladders
- ❏ lint-free dust cloths
- ❏ masking tape and tape dispenser
- ❏ razor blades

## Cleaning tools

Most painting tools can be cleaned first by soaking in turps (white spirit) if oil-based, then by washing in hot, soapy water. If using water-based paints, hot soapy water followed by rinsing will do the trick. Rinse thoroughly – tools will harden and become useless if any paint residue is left after washing.

All brushes must be carefully rinsed after use. Have two or three tins of turps (white spirit) ready to use.

To soften a hardened brush, dip it into a saucepan of boiling water, detergent and ammonia – or immerse in paint stripper or brush cleaner for a short time.

## The work area

The ideal work area is light, airy and spacious – with lots of shelving, cupboards and storage space. If this sounds too idyllic for your circumstances, don't despair – you can also get by with a very basic set-up.

If you are short on space, an efficient work area can be created by fitting out a cupboard with shelves and using a card table which can be folded away when necessary.

Remember, too, that many of the painting and varnishing materials that you will be using are highly flammable – so if you set up work in your kitchen, stay well away from the cooking area.

Ventilation is very important – you need a constant flow of fresh air to disperse any potentially dangerous fumes.

Keep your work area as clean as possible – stray dust and grime can ruin a freshly painted surface.

Good lighting is essential. Fit an extra light overhead if you don't have good natural light.

A set of shelves close at hand is an extra bonus for storage of tools and supplies which you need to lay your hands on quickly and easily.

## Preparation

Preparation is crucial to a successful result. All walls should be sanded back and, where necessary, filled.

A wonderful filler for large holes in walls is cornice glue. This is in powder form and may be bought in bulk and made up following the instructions on the packet. It sands beautifully, so the patching is not evident. If this is not obtainable, any good wall filler will do the job.

Once the filler is dry and sanded so that the filling is imperceptible, the filled area must be sealed. If you do not seal the filled area, you will find it shows through as a grey patch when you apply the wall glaze.

Shellac is a sealing medium. It is thinned with methylated spirits and dries almost immediately, so that you can get on with the painting job straight away. If shellac is not available, use whatever sealer you can buy at your local suppliers. It is most important that the walls are well sanded and made as smooth as possible.

Once the wall is in as good a condition as you can possibly achieve and all sanding has been completed, wipe down with calico rags and vacuum the floor and walls. Then wipe all over with tack rags. These are made of cheesecloth, impregnated with linseed oil, and are invaluable for removing dust.

Before painting the walls, make sure that you mask all areas which are not to be painted – this will save hours of cleaning up later. Only buy good quality masking tape – never buy masking tape which does not bear a brand name or which is on sale because it is old stock.

## Wall glazing

If you are restoring old walls – or new ones for that matter – great care must be given to the preparation. As with so many aspects

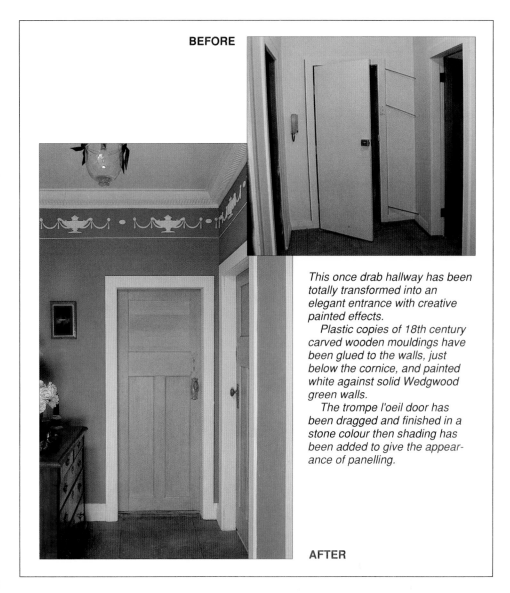

BEFORE

AFTER

*This once drab hallway has been totally transformed into an elegant entrance with creative painted effects.*

*Plastic copies of 18th century carved wooden mouldings have been glued to the walls, just below the cornice, and painted white against solid Wedgwood green walls.*

*The trompe l'oeil door has been dragged and finished in a stone colour then shading has been added to give the appearance of panelling.*

of interior and exterior decoration, the better the preparation, the better the final result.

You may now start painting the walls with eggshell sheen enamel. (The colour is up to you, but generally a room or a whole house can happily be prepared in white eggshell sheen enamel and then any colour or colours imposed over the white.) If you cannot buy this style of paint, you can easily make it yourself by mixing one part matt/flat enamel with one part satin enamel, thus creating the slight sheen one sees on an eggshell.

If you do not wish to work in oil-based paints, you can make the same eggshell sheen using acrylic house paints. However, a word of warning: when applying a decorative paint glaze to walls, the glaze is more workable and stays 'open' (does not dry out immediately) longer if it is imposed on an oil-based paint rather than on an acrylic paint. Acrylic paints are very absorbent and tend to soak up a decorative paint glaze in a very thirsty manner and make it much more difficult to work.

When applying the paint to the walls, you can use a brush or a roller. Rollers are very quick, but tend to leave behind the appearance of an orange skin. To overcome this orange-peel effect, lay on one section with the roller – about 610 mm at a time then quickly come back over the wet paint with a good bristle brush and 'lay-off', that is, pull the brush from the ceiling down to the skirting board through the paint, removing the orange-peel pattern in the paint. If you do this carefully the paint surface should be absolutely smooth.

Doors, architraves, skirting boards, windows, etc, should be prepared in the same way, using a brush to apply the paint. After the application of two coats of eggshell sheen enamel the walls may look opaque. If this is the case, you are then ready to get on with the decorative glaze. If, however, there are patches on the wall which have a slightly grey appearance, you must apply more coats of eggshell sheen until the wall is absolutely opaque.

Once the walls are a solid colour, they are ready to receive the decorative glaze. One word of warning here: if, in spite of all

your hard work, you have not been able to achieve an absolutely even, smooth surface on your walls, there are some glazes which will not be suitable. For instance, the dragged finish requires a very smooth, even surface, allowing the brush to glide over the wall without meeting any bumps.

Before applying your decorative glaze you must mask skirting boards, cornices, architraves and doors if you are to achieve a first-class, professional finish. Use a low-tack tape, made for French polishers, which is half low-tack and the other half brown paper. The half that is brown paper will provide extra protection to the masked areas. Be careful at the corners where it does not bond well to itself; you will need a length of ordinary tape over it to make sure the bonding is secure at that point.

Taking the trouble to mask off

areas properly is well worth the effort. Your finish will be crisp and clean on all the edges and you will have no cleaning up to do. Ignore this step and you will spend many tedious hours removing unwanted paint.

Before commencing work on the walls, spend some time practising on sample boards so that you get the feel of creating the paint finish. If you have a wall or two on which to practise, such as a lavatory or laundry area (they can always be repainted!), try the finish on those walls before embarking on a more ambitious project.

## Woodwork

In Victorian and Edwardian houses, the colour in woodwork was often made by aniline dyes suspended in either shellac or varnish. This dye will bleed through almost any paint finish.

To determine if the colour is, in fact, aniline, take some steel wool and methylated spirits and rub the finish vigorously. If the

*This once raw concrete floor has been painted to suit the soft colours and textures of the room and to give the impression of stone-tiling.*
*The concrete was first sealed with shellac, then three colours were ragged and sponged on to create the texture and appearance of stone.*
*The floor was then finished with 'lining' to make the tiling pattern.*

finish starts to come away and some colour appears to be remaining in the wood, you can be sure it is aniline. Similarly, if the finish is varnish with aniline, steel wool soaked in turps (white spirit) used in the same way will give you the same answer.

The only material which will contain these dyes is an aluminium paint. This paint is readily available for painting roofs and is invaluable for covering aniline. Follow the directions on the tin for application. Make sure the background is completely covered with the aluminium paint before proceeding to the next step of applying the eggshell sheen enamel.

## Furniture

If the piece of furniture has been well painted, varnished or French polished, there is no need to strip it. If, however, it is a mess of dripping paint, remove the offending cover first.

If the first case applies, sand back the piece until it is smooth.

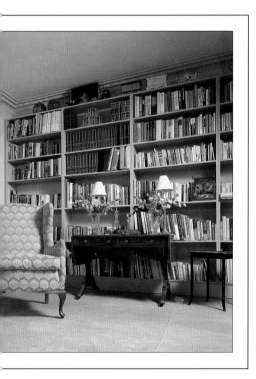

Fill any areas which require filling, then seal filled areas with shellac or a proprietary sealer. Sand the sealed area until it is smooth, wipe with a calico rag and then a tack cloth, and then begin painting with either oil or acrylic eggshell sheen enamel, usually white.

If the piece of furniture has been stripped, then it must be treated as raw and first sealed with shellac or a proprietary sealer. Sand as above and wipe off – then coat with the usual coats of eggshell sheen enamel to an opaque coverage.

You are then ready to apply the decorative paint glaze.

## Glazes

In painted finishes, glaze does not mean shiny. A glaze is a semi-translucent coat of paint painted onto an opaque background. The paint is broken open with a tool, such as a cloth, plastic bag or brush, allowing the opaque background to shine through, thus creating depth and dimension. Consequently, these finishes are often referred to as 'broken' paint finishes. If you wish to have a shine on the finish, this is done by applying varnish – either satin or gloss.

Varnish is the final coat that gives protection and an extra depth to painted finishes, depending on the number of coats applied. Of the many types of varnish available, gloss marine varnish offers the most protection. When matured and wet-sanded it has a smooth surface that withstands heat very well. Marine satin and matt/flat varnishes are also hardy finishes, as are the old-fashioned resin-

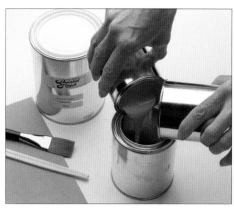

*Mixing the eggshell sheen enamel*

*Applying the eggshell sheen enamel*

based varnishes.

Most varnishes tend to yellow slightly, but some can be deliberately tinted to correct this. Some yellowing is fine over most colours except white and pale pastels. A little umber mixed in varnish to be applied over a red antiquing glaze gives an excellent result.

Surfaces in constant use require a great deal of protection and can be varnished in a number of ways, depending on the desired appearance. All varnishes, particularly high gloss, should be left to mature.

## Scumble medium or antiquing glaze

Scumble medium is a semi-translucent medium composed of linseed oil, turps (white spirit), whiting and extenders to create a longer drying time.

Scumble medium is an essential part of glazing. It adds translucency to the paint, extends the drying time – which means you have more time to work with the paint once it has been applied –and enables the paint to hold the imprint of the tool. If you did not use scumble medium and performed, say, a stipple, you would find the paint had closed up into an opaque colour within an hour or two.

Oil-based and water-based scumble medium have the same characteristics, although obviously made from entirely different materials.

*To prepare for stippling apply the glaze to the skirting board*

*Bounce the brush up and down into the glaze to create a stippled effect*

# Stippling

If using water-based mediums, add one part glaze to two parts water. You must always use your common sense when thinning, as the viscosity of paint and scumble medium can vary dramatically. The glaze should always sit on the background as a cover not a texture. If you find there is texture in the glaze, it is too thick and you will need to thin it.

It is recommended that stippling is kept for the smaller areas of a room. One of the most difficult finishes to perform expertly is a stippled wall. Stippled doors, skirting boards, architraves and cornices look wonderful.

### MATERIALS

- ☐ one part matt/flat enamel
- ☐ one part scumble medium
- ☐ one or two parts turps (white spirit)

### SPECIAL TOOLS NEEDED

- ☐ roller or brush to apply the glaze
- ☐ rectangular wall stipple brush

### METHOD

1 Quickly apply the glaze to the background, leaving a ragged edge (this is in case the edge dries out and you get a seam line – a ragged seam line is less obvious than a straight join).

2 Now bounce the brush up and down into the glaze. Keep wiping off the brush so that any excess glaze is removed from the brush and not returned to the paint surface.

3 When the area is completed, remove the masking tape and allow the glaze to dry overnight. The result is the soft look of an unvarnished finish. If desired, a coat or two of satin varnish may be applied.

# Dragging

The technique of dragging is perfect for doors, skirting boards and architraves. If working on such architectural timber, use a 50 mm cutting-in brush (house-painter's brush). A plain door can be transformed into a panelled piece, simply by masking out each panel, dragging and then moving on to the next section.

*To prepare for dragging, use a paint roller to roll the glaze on evenly*

*Jam the dragging brush into the glaze, feathering the brush out away from the surface you are working on*

### MATERIALS

**Oil-based glaze:**
- ☐ one part matt/flat enamel
- ☐ one part scumble medium
- ☐ one to two parts turps (white spirit)

**Water-based glaze:**
- ☐ two parts acrylic paint
- ☐ one part water-based scumble medium (don't use water unless the glaze is very thick)

### SPECIAL TOOLS NEEDED

- ☐ roller to apply glaze
- ☐ wall-dragging brush with strong bristles

### METHOD

1 Dragging requires two people working: one to apply the glaze with a roller and the other to work up the ladder. Roll the glaze evenly onto the wall in strips about 900 mm wide. Roll the outside edge constantly so that the glaze doesn't get a dry edge – this shows as a darker stripe.

2 Jam the dragging brush into the glaze between the cornice and wall and then evenly drag down the wall. If you are

on a ladder, just walk down the ladder without hesitating – hesitations will cause irregular stop-marks in the finish.

3 As you work down towards the skirting board, feather the brush out, away from the wall. Wipe the brush, turn it over to the other side, jam it into the glaze at the skirting board and pull it up the wall over the same area you have just dragged down.

4 Feather away from the wall near the cornice. This should be enough for good, strong drag marks. Continue around the room until each wall has been dragged.

# Sponging

Low contrast is best for this finish, otherwise the room can look as though a demented animal has run across the walls! It is essential that you use real sea sponges as they impart a soft, subtle shape not possible with synthetic sponges.

## MATERIALS

**Oil-based glaze:**
- ☐ one part matt/flat enamel
- ☐ one part scumble medium
- ☐ one to two parts turps (white spirit)

**Water-based glaze:**
- ☐ one part matt/flat acrylic
- ☐ one part water scumble
- ☐ three parts or more water

SPECIAL TOOLS NEEDED
- ☐ sea sponges
- ☐ 50 mm cutting-in brush
- ☐ round stipple brush

## METHOD

1 Dip the sponges in water and wring them out – this makes them soft and malleable. Load one sponge with the glaze and apply to the wall in a random pattern – working an area about 900 mm wide at a time from floor to ceiling.

2 Dip a second sponge into turps (white spirit), or water if using a water-based glaze, and start to soften the harsh edges of the glaze. Move the glaze around a little, taking some into the background space where there is no glaze at all. This creates a feeling of depth, and creates another tone. Make sure that you work quickly and do not allow the glaze to dry up or you will have harsh join marks where you apply the next section.

3 Corners are a little tricky and it is wise to use a cutting-in brush or a round stipple brush to help you get into the join. The last thing you want is a strong white line running down the corners of the room. If you think the finish is too strong, follow up with an overglaze (see page 40).

# Parchment Finish

This finish is best performed with the second glaze in oil-based paint and mediums. It requires two processes, but can be completed in one day. It gives a lovely, textured effect to the walls.

## MATERIALS

**First glaze:**
- ☐ thick white acrylic paint, straight out of the tin

**Second glaze:**
- ☐ one part oil-based paint
- ☐ one part scumble medium
- ☐ one part turps (white spirit)

*Above left: To prepare for sponging load one sponge with glaze and apply it randomly*
*Left: Dip a second sponge into turps (white spirit) or water (if using a water-based glaze), and use it to soften the first glaze*

SPECIAL TOOLS NEEDED
- ☐ 75 mm bristle brush
- ☐ washed lint-free calico rags

## METHOD

1 Take the bristle brush and apply the first glaze to the wall in a random, slightly basket-weave pattern. Allow as many brushstrokes as possible to remain in the paint.

2 Take a rag which has been wrung out in water, and move the paint around slightly, taking some into the previously untouched area. When you have finished, most of the wall should have varying areas of paint on it. There should be about 15 per cent only where the background is showing through. Allow to dry for one to two hours.

3 Take another rag and dip into the second glaze. Apply to the wall, patting on and rubbing, using a circular swirling motion. If you find you have applied too much glaze, or it is too dark, dip another cloth into turps (white spirit) and remove some glaze.

4 When dry, this finish has texture and irregular areas of colour where the first glaze has sopped up the second glaze. Make sure your application is reasonably even so that you do not have too much variation in the degree of colour.

# Crackle Finish

## MATERIALS
- ☐ eggshell sheen enamel
- ☐ masking tape
- ☐ matt/flat acrylic paint
- ☐ crackle medium

## SPECIAL TOOLS NEEDED
- ☐ brush and/or ruler
- ☐ plant sprayer and water
- ☐ oil-based or water-based varnish

## METHOD

1 The furniture to be decorated must be prepared with as many coats of background colour in eggshell sheen enamel (or eggshell acrylic) as are needed to be opaque. It is essential that the background is not porous and the background paint is absolutely dry before crackle medium is applied.

**2** If you intend to use the crackle medium as an inset, such as on these drawers, first mask out the area with masking tape. Once the tape is down (always run your thumbnail along the edge to ensure good bonding), apply the crackle medium. It is viscous and should be allowed to flow onto the surface rather than be painted on in the normal manner.

**3** Make sure that the piece is horizontal, as the medium runs if on an angle and can make a mess. Allow the medium to dry. This can take from one to two hours to

*To complete the chest of drawers shown on page 36, first mask out the area for crackling with masking tape*

*Apply the crackle medium, allow it to dry, cover with the paint, then lightly mist with a fine water spray*

*Cut out the masking tape with a blade or you risk peeling off the newly painted finish*

overnight, depending on the weather. Don't proceed to the next step until you are sure the medium is absolutely dry (it dries very flat and is often hard to see).

**4** The paint used over the medium must be matt/flat acrylic. You can use a household acrylic paint, but sometimes good quality artist's acrylics are even better. Often a deep-tint base household paint will not crack so well because it is too heavily pigmented. You need to try your paint and medium on a sample board first. If you want coarse, graphic crackling, use the paint straight out of the tin, with random brushstrokes. There must be no pressure on the brush. The loaded brush must glide over the medium. Keep reloading the brush. Crackling occurs in the direction of the brushstrokes.

**5** If you want the fine, cobwebby crackling to show, thin the paint approximately two parts paint to one part water. Once you place the loaded brush, or roller (for ease of application in this instance), on the dried crackle medium surface, it must merely glide over the surface and be reloaded constantly. Speed is of the essence. So, very quickly apply the loaded brush to the surface, keep reloading and reapplying, using absolutely no pressure. Having applied all over, cover with the paint then lightly mist three to four times with a fine mist of water from a plant sprayer.

**6** The crackling occurs as the paint dries, which is almost immediately. If you wish to protect this finish, use oil-based or water-based varnish. Water-based varnish can reactivate the crackle medium, so be careful not to overwork it. However, once dry and matured for a few days, water-based paint is very strong and, unless the piece of furniture receives a lot of wear, it is not essential to varnish.

**7** A fabulous crackled, aged surface can be obtained on walls by using this medium. To be held satisfactorily on a vertical surface, the medium must be thinned one part crackle medium to one part water. It can then be painted onto a wall (must be non-porous) and will dry without running.

**8** The big trick with this wall finish is that the acrylic paint which is used over the top of the medium must be thick, otherwise crackling will not occur over the thinned crackle medium.

**9** Once the medium is absolutely dry, the acrylic paint may be applied. It looks best if random brushstrokes are used and, again, the brush must glide over the surface so that the crackle medium beneath is not disturbed. In this case, the paint should be applied with a brush, not a roller. Crackling usually occurs in the direction of the brushstrokes, so bear this in mind as you work. Don't forget to cut out the masking tape with a blade, or you will peel the finish off the wall.

# Overglaze

This will soften or brighten a finish.

MATERIALS

**Oil-based glaze:**
- ☐ one part matt/flat enamel
- ☐ one part scumble medium
- ☐ one or two parts turps (white spirit)

**Water-based glaze:**
- ☐ two parts acrylic paint
- ☐ one part water-based scumble medium (don't use water unless the glaze is very thick)

SPECIAL TOOLS NEEDED
- ☐ brush or roller
- ☐ stipple brush
- ☐ pieces of lint-free calico

METHOD

**1** The finish on which you wish to apply the overglaze should have been allowed to dry overnight. Apply the overglaze with a brush or a roller, stippling to remove any brush or roller strokes, and then start texturing with a piece of washed, lint-free calico.

**2** Allow some of the background to shine through. Do not cover the background completely with the overglaze – the application is simply to soften or enliven. Make sure you pick up any drips with the calico.

**3** The overglaze will be absorbed into the background quite easily and you will find it adds a lovely amorphous quality to the original glaze.

**4** Oil-based scumble medium is sensitive to ultraviolet light in that it yellows if covered. If you wish to move your pictures after they have been hung for a year or so, you may find that there are yellow patches on the wall. Once these areas are again exposed to ultraviolet light, these yellow patches will disappear in about a month. The same applies to a furniture surface which has been finished with the scumble medium.

# Ragging

MATERIALS
- [ ] base coat
- [ ] oil-based top coat (see Parchment Finish)
- [ ] turps (white spirit)

SPECIAL TOOLS NEEDED
- [ ] brush or roller
- [ ] lint-free cotton rags

METHOD
This is a very quick and effective way to achieve an interesting effect on a plain wall, using a scrunched-up, lint-free rag or even a plastic bag.

*Top: Apply the darker colour to the surface to be painted*
*Above: Before the paint dries, break up and lift off the colour using a scrunched up clean, lint-free rag, leaving behind the ragging effect*

1 You may find some team effort worth while here, as the effect depends on the top coat of paint being 'lifted off' just after it is applied. While one person is painting the top coat, the other member of the team can follow behind doing the ragging. If the top coat is allowed to dry too much, the effect will be spoiled as not enough of the base coat will show through after ragging.

2 Just after the top coat is applied, it is 'lifted off' by dabbing with a rag or something similar, exposing the base colour and creating an interesting crushed effect. The base coat can be of emulsion or acrylic paint or oil-based. Oil-based paints give a richer look than emulsion.

3 For the top coat, use oil-based paint thinned with turps (white spirit), or emulsion or acrylic paint, thinned with water. You can contrast colours or tones of the same colour, by applying a top coat that is darker than the base.

# Simple Marbling

Marbled skirting boards can become a very attractive, decorative feature in an otherwise simple or understated room.

MATERIALS
**Oil-based glaze:**
- [ ] one part matt/flat enamel
- [ ] one part scumble medium
- [ ] one part turps (white spirit)

**Water-based glaze:**
- [ ] one part matt/flat acrylic
- [ ] one part water-based scumble medium
- [ ] one part water

SPECIAL TOOLS NEEDED
- [ ] 50 mm cutting-in brush
- [ ] 50 mm round stipple brush
- [ ] feather
- [ ] newspaper

METHOD
1 If you are working in a room 3m x 3m, you will need about forty pieces of tabloid newspaper. Fold each piece in half diagonally and then fold each side into a series of 25 mm concertinas.

2 Paint the glaze onto the skirting board and quickly stipple to remove the brushstrokes. Now, with an up-and-down movement of the newspaper, break open

*Paint the glaze onto the skirting board and quickly stipple to remove any brushstrokes*

*Using an up-and-down movement, work with newspaper, folded in concertina fashion, to break open the glaze, revealing the pale paint base beneath*

*Work over the fractured area with a feather, loaded with a little white glaze, to make a pattern of veins in the marble*

the glaze to reveal the pale paint base beneath. Move the paper sideways on the glaze, thus creating fractures, leaving virtually none of the surface untouched. The trick with this is that all the surface has movement to it.

3 Make sure that the finish runs at a diagonal of about 45° – it must not be upright. As each piece of newspaper becomes clogged with glaze, discard it. When the whole area is fractured, you can work it over with a feather, loaded with a little white glaze to add some veins. However, this finish will stand out very well on its own without the application of the veins.

# Stencilling

*Stencilling is one of the oldest decorative effects and can be as simple or ornate as you wish. Traditionally, stencils were cut from oiled cardboard or even brass sheets and were regarded as a craftsman's tools. Today you can still use brass and cardboard stencils but inexpensive plastic stencils are now readily available in an enormous variety of contemporary and traditional designs. You can also design and cut your own stencil using a plastic sheet and tracing your chosen design with a chinagraph pencil or a fine, indelible, felt-tipped pen.*

## Before You Begin

❑ It is important to use the correct brush for stencilling – an ordinary paint brush will not do. Stencil brushes are flat-topped and are used by dabbing the brush down onto the area to be coloured, rather than stroking. This prevents paint being pushed under the stencil edges and smearing the design. You can use small natural sponges.

❑ As for your paints, it is best to use acrylic or special fast-drying stencil paint. If mixing colours to achieve a desired tint, mix enough for the entire room, as it is difficult to duplicate a particular colour mix. Take care too that your paints are very creamy in consistency, so they will not clog the brush or sponge, but not so thin that they will run under the stencil edges. If you are stencilling in more than one colour and are concerned that the colours should not run into one another, paints can be dried quickly with a hairdryer on low force and medium heat.

❑ If stencilling with more than one colour, it is a good idea to cover with masking tape those parts of the stencil design to be painted in the second colour. Wait for the first colour to dry before stencilling with the second one and so on. This will stop one colour from bleeding into the other.

*Top: Applying the first colour of the stencilled border to the wall*
*Above: Applying the second colour to complete the stencilled design*

# Stencilling a Border

MATERIALS

- [ ] suitable paint
- [ ] stencil brushes
- [ ] manila cards
- [ ] linseed oil
- [ ] turps (white spirit)
- [ ] sharp craft knife
- [ ] cutting board
- [ ] pencils
- [ ] plumb line
- [ ] spirit level
- [ ] chalk
- [ ] masking tape

METHOD

Make the stencil in the same way as for the Stencilled Floorcloth on page 56.

1 Paint the wall in the normal way. Then, using a plumb line and spirit level, mark the position of your border, marking both horizontal and vertical base lines.

2 Place the stencil on the wall, aligning its edges with the drawn lines and marking each corner of the stencil with easily-removed blackboard chalk. Continue placing the stencil along the guidelines, marking the corners along the entire length of the border.

3 Attach the stencil to the wall with masking tape. If you are using more than one colour, cover over any areas to be painted in another colour with masking tape to avoid paint overlapping.

4 Be sure to remove any excess paint from your brush or sponge before applying it to the wall. You will find surprisingly little paint is needed. Work in circular movements from the centre of each cutout area to the edges. Part of the charm of a stencilled decoration is the variations that occur in paint application, so don't feel compelled to paint until a solid block of colour appears, or to match one motif exactly to the next.

5 When the paint is dry, unmask the stencil and clean it if necessary. Then move the stencil to the next set of chalk marks and paint as before. Continue in this way until the border is completed.

*Use this stencil design at any size you like. Simply enlarge it on a photocopying machine to your preferred size*

# Decorating with Wallpaper

There are not many do-it-yourself activities that will give you more satisfaction than wallpapering. And it really is easy!

Vinyl-based wallpapers (which come prepasted and ready to put straight on the wall) make paper-hanging so easy that even first-timers can produce quite professional results.

Wallpapering is particularly satisfying because the rewards are so immediate and dramatic. In just a day or two you can transform a tired bedroom, a bland living room or a problem hallway. What's more, the wallpaper comes off the wall as easily as it went on, so in a few years if you feel like a change – hey presto and it's a whole new look.

Use wallpapers and borders to inject life, colour, warmth and style into the gloomiest of rooms. Create a feeling of coolness in a room that becomes overheated easily and add warmth and cosiness to rooms that miss out on the sunlight.

Let your lifestyle and individual sense of design help you choose your wallpapers – and what a choice! Whether you are looking for a sophisticated city-style look for a new flat or a country cottage look for a house, there's a huge range of superb designs to cater for your taste. You can mix patterns and plains or even florals with stripes, paper below the chair rail or above it! It's up to you. One thing is certain – you'll have lots of fun!

## How to choose your wallpaper

Most shops carry large 'libraries' of pattern books with entire ranges in a variety of colourways. However, you don't want to spend hours and days wading through sample books. This usually leads to confusion and much frustration!

Instead, take details of the rooms to be decorated, including their size; colour and style of the drapes, carpets and other furnishings; the direction windows face; colours of adjoining rooms. A good retailer will be able to show you an imaginative range of options. Don't be afraid to select something that reflects your personality and individuality. You could try one of the superb flocks: brilliant if you're lucky enough to have a chandelier. You might prefer a grasscloth – real or imitation – with its horizontal weave and texture which creates the illusion of the room being larger than it really is.

Still not sure? As well as pattern books, many retailers carry stocks of sample rolls and may allow you to take these home to see how the paper looks in the room it is destined for.

## WHICH WALLPAPER TO CHOOSE?

❏ **Vinyl** is today's most popular wallpaper. Made from polyvinyl chloride (PVC) it is resistant to water and can be scrubbed with a soft bristle brush to remove most marks. It is usually prepasted.

❏ **Vinyl coated** papers have had liquid PVC applied to them, giving a more durable, washable surface.

❏ **Embossed vinyl** has been moulded to give a raised pattern and has a tough paper backing.

❏ **Blown vinyl** has a relief design effect, created by expanding the vinyl during manufacture.

❏ **Duplex** wallcovering consists of two sheets of paper which have been bonded for strength. It can be sponged but not scrubbed.

❏ **Natural papers**, such as grasscloth and silks, cork, wood veneers, burlap, are all made from natural materials applied to paper backings. Hanging them usually requires some degree of expertise.

❏ **Flock wallcoverings** are regarded as an elegant background for traditional decorating schemes. Finely chopped wool, rayon or nylon is applied to the design and coated with adhesive, for a luxurious velvet effect.

❏ **Relief papers** are usually white and not to be confused with the embossed vinyls or flocks. Relief papers include anaglypta, a great favourite in Victorian times. Anaglypta is made by bonding two sheets of paper then passing it through deeply-embossed rollers.

❏ **Mylar foil** is made from a resin. It looks like real foil but won't show creases after hanging.

❏ **Foil** is a thin, flexible metal sheet (often aluminium), laminated onto a backing of paper or fabric. Excellent for accent areas such as one wall of a bathroom or in a small hallway.

❏ **Murals** range from maps of the world to scenes of autumnal forests and tropical islands which can cover an entire wall, creating a feeling of spaciousness in small rooms.

# Getting Started

Preparing the surface is important and well worth the effort. You should aim for clean, non-porous surfaces because porous surfaces 'steal' moisture from the paste, affecting its adhesive qualities. Different wall surfaces will require different kinds of preparation. Check with your local wallpaper shop for any specific instructions for your walls.

If possible, remove blinds and curtains, wall lights and, of course, prints and pictures! Give yourself the maximum room in which to work by moving furniture to another room or placing it in the centre. Use drop sheets to protect your floor coverings: old bed sheets are ideal.

If you intend papering the ceiling as well as the walls, do this first. If not, paint the ceiling and all woodwork before you begin papering.

## Which room first?

Most people wallpapering for the first time choose a small room, such as the bathroom, in which to start...just in case! This is a mistake – you'll have a cistern, shower recess, bath, wash basin, cabinet and all sorts of other odd-shaped fittings to contend with and work around.

It's much easier to begin in a bedroom or lounge where the walls are uninterrupted, allowing you to quickly polish your skills. By the time you reach the bathroom, you'll be an expert!

## Borders

Friezes or borders are very popular and have led to a revival of interest in all wallcoverings. To begin with, borders are inexpensive and simple to apply and remove. Success with a border will inspire a feeling of confidence and soon you'll want to paper an entire room.

The tools you'll need are the same as for wallpapering and the same rules apply for wall preparation as for wallpaper.

Measuring is easy too. It's all done in linear metres, so you simply measure the distance around a room. If it is going around a door, then measure the sides and top too. Most borders are sold in 5 or 10 m lengths so

Lifestyle

you get plenty for your money! They are often prepasted so you can use the water trough as you would with full-sized wallpaper.

Perhaps the most dramatic use of borders is at chair rail height. You can then paper below and paint above or vice-versa, or use two different but complementary wallpapers and have the border intersecting them.

You can apply a border over the top of wallpaper to provide focal points, or use a border to give added importance to a prized mirror, painting or print. You can even apply them to ceilings for a very distinctive designer look!

## How much wallpaper do you need?

| Walls | | Distance around the room (doors and windows included) | | | | | | | | | | | | | | | | | | |
|---|---|---|---|---|---|---|---|---|---|---|---|---|---|---|---|---|---|---|---|---|
| **METRES** | | 8.53 | 9.75 | 10.97 | 12.19 | 13.41 | 14.63 | 15.85 | 17.07 | 18.29 | 19.51 | 20.73 | 21.95 | 23.16 | 24.38 | 25.60 | 26.82 | 28.04 | 29.26 |
| | **FEET** | 28' | 32' | 36' | 40' | 44' | 48' | 52' | 56' | 60' | 64' | 68' | 72' | 76' | 80' | 84' | 88' | 92' | 96' |
| 2.13 to 2.29 | 6' 10" to 7' 6" | 5 | 5 | 6 | 6 | 7 | 7 | 8 | 8 | 9 | 9 | 10 | 10 | 10 | 11 | 11 | 13 | 13 | 14 |
| 2.30 to 2.44 | 7' 7" to 8' 0" | 5 | 5 | 6 | 6 | 7 | 7 | 8 | 9 | 9 | 10 | 10 | 11 | 11 | 12 | 13 | 14 | 14 | 15 |
| 2.45 to 2.59 | 8' 1" to 8' 6" | 5 | 6 | 6 | 7 | 7 | 8 | 8 | 9 | 9 | 10 | 10 | 12 | 12 | 13 | 14 | 15 | 15 | 15 |
| 2.60 to 2.74 | 8' 7" to 9' 0" | 5 | 6 | 6 | 7 | 7 | 8 | 9 | 9 | 10 | 10 | 11 | 13 | 13 | 14 | 14 | 15 | 15 | 16 |
| 2.75 to 2.90 | 9' 1" to 9' 6" | 5 | 6 | 7 | 7 | 8 | 8 | 9 | 10 | 10 | 11 | 11 | 13 | 14 | 14 | 15 | 15 | 16 | 17 |
| 2.91 to 3.05 | 9' 7" to 10' 0" | 6 | 6 | 7 | 8 | 8 | 9 | 10 | 10 | 11 | 11 | 12 | 14 | 14 | 15 | 16 | 16 | 17 | 17 |
| 3.06 to 3.20 | 10' 1" to 11' 6" | 6 | 6 | 7 | 8 | 9 | 9 | 10 | 11 | 11 | 12 | 13 | 14 | 15 | 16 | 16 | 17 | 18 | 18 |
| | | Number of rolls required | | | | | | | | | | | | | | | | | |

# A Roomful of Treasures

Long ago you were given a blue plate, then you bought another one at a local bazaar and then a friend gave you one for Christmas and, before you knew it, you had a collection! Your collection of plates, dolls, jelly moulds, tin cans, or whatever, offers great decorating possibilities if you display it well.

Perhaps you're a traveller and have brought back souvenirs that share a common theme – scarves, plates, luggage labels – you can frame or hang them on a dull wall. Ethnic collections can bring fascinating textures and colour to a room. Hand-loomed fabrics and carpets, primitive sculpture and hand-woven baskets will all complement each other.

Try to create a theme in certain rooms. An old favourite is a marine theme in bathrooms – shells collected from holidays long ago, framed shell prints and perhaps a mirror surrounded by shells. Libraries and studios lend themselves to collections of photographs, sporting trophies or memorabilia, and old prints. Kitchens are ideal for displaying utensils – old jelly moulds, ornate cake plates, bottle openers, scales with weights and measures, beverage bottles and old stoneware jars, all bring a rustic, cared-for and friendly look to a kitchen. If you are lucky enough to own one, an old timber dresser makes an ideal home for a kitchen collection. Collections of quite large objects, such as copper pans or baskets, can look wonderful suspended from the ceiling on hooks.

*Above: A lovely collection of old millefleurs plates brings warmth to a plain white wall. See how the variety in shape and size adds interest to the display*
*Below: Kitchen ceilings are not usually very interesting to look at, except if they are like this one. A collection of stoneware milk jugs is suspended from timber beams*

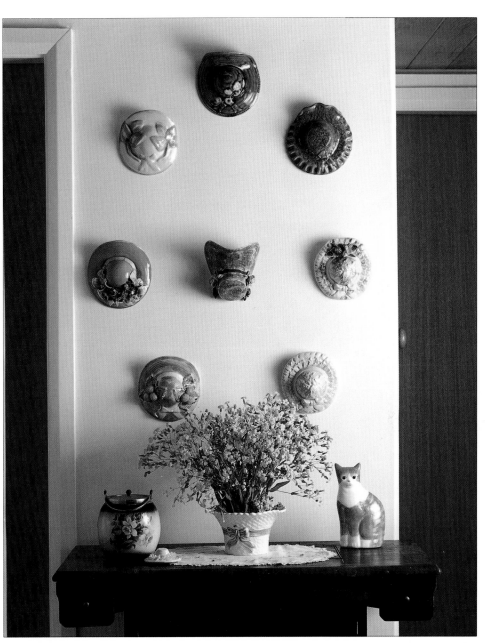

*Top: A collection of antique ginger beer bottles line open shelves in a country-style kitchen. The warmth and colours of the stoneware add a pleasing feature to the room*
*Above: For a great sense of fun why not a collection of old keys of various shapes and sizes? Collected from junk shops, attics and church bazaars, they are mounted on a simple board using cup hooks*

Collections in entrance halls make a great decorating statement. This is often the first impression visitors get about the owners of the house and your first chance to show off! Our photograph of old-fashioned vases, shaped like hats, shows a colourful and whimsical touch, especially when complemented by a large bunch of spring blooms in a quaint old jug. Take care though, if you have small children and a large dog, a table in the narrow entrance hall may not be the ideal place to display a precious collection of china.

*Above: This is a truly charming and unusual collection of vases in the shape of fancy hats, carefully mounted on a plain wall*

Some collections just evolve, or you can set out quite deliberately to assemble objects in a decorative group. Sometimes items from different eras can be combined successfully, but keep a colour or theme link between them. Old theatre programmes, nautical bits and pieces, books, paintings of a particular subject, coloured china, fashion accessories or toys are all varied and delightful when gathered and displayed in interesting collections.

48

# Framing Up

Bare walls just cry out for the decorator's touch and pictures are the obvious solution. The right frame for your picture and the arrangement of a group of plates can make all the difference. These are some very clever decorator's tricks for framing your prints or paintings.

*Above: This charming collection of old black and white prints is not what it seems. If you look closely, you will see that the pictures, the frames and the ornate hanging bows and drapes are in fact applied directly to the wall*
*Left: Give new life to an old picture frame rescued from the junk shop with the use of a little gold paint and some fancy ribbon*
*Above centre: Another frame salvaged from the junk heap hides behind this border of glued-on shells*
*Above left: Frame a group of china plates by stencilling a pattern of bows and tassels on the wall behind*
*Far left: Follow through the folk-art theme of these hand-stitched samplers with rustic styled frames like these. It is important that your frame reflects the style and feeling of the art*

# *what's* Afoot?

*W*hatever you choose for floor coverings, it will be a substantial investment, so don't rush into it. Quality ranges from the very basic to the luxurious, and there are attractive options at both ends of the scale and in between.

# All about Floors

## Carpets

Laying fitted carpets (wall-to-wall or broadloom) should be left to professional carpet layers but large carpet squares, rugs and carpet tiles are portable, easy to lay and can be repositioned to spread the wear. Fibres can be man-made or natural: acrylic and polyester, nylon, wool or wool blends. Nylon is durable and versatile, wool is a natural insulator and less prone to static electricity; stains, dust and burns are less noticeable. Popular wool-nylon blends display the advantages of both fibres. Pile also affects wear and appearance. Loop-pile is tougher than the plush surface of beautiful cut-pile carpets which mark easily. Combination cut-and-loop or sturdy cut-and-twist offer interesting patterns and textures. Modern, easy-care rubber-backed carpets are available in attractive colours and patterns featuring a variable density of pile for different purposes. They're durable and comfortable to stand on.

*Right: Slate floors in one of the many beautiful colours available are an ideal choice for a kitchen floor*
*Below: Pure wool fitted carpet enhances the open plan of this lovely living/dining room*

## Ceramic tiles

This is the perfect choice for anyone needing a low maintenance, easy-to-clean flooring but their highly glazed surface may be slippery when wet, something to remember when choosing bathroom or kitchen tiles. Ceramic tiles retain heat in winter yet stay deliciously cool in summer. They come in different sizes, from the very small to the very large. Generally, large tiles should be installed by professionals, as should those on awkward floors where you need to cut tiles to fit around built-in units and plumbing. The amount you save by laying them yourself can easily be swallowed up in the cost of replacing badly cut or damaged tiles. Remember too, that ceramic tiles give you no second chance for that dropped plate or vase. If you are a bit of a 'butter fingers' or have small children, this may not be a wise choice for you.

## Slate

The colours and textures of slate enhance any setting. It stays cool in summer and warm in winter. You'll need a diamond-tipped saw to cut slate but its irregular texture will camouflage accidents. You must allow time for slate bedded in sand and cement to dry thoroughly, then sweep away mineral salts before sealing. Clean with a mop and warm water.

Above: For a truly dramatic effect, you can lay ceramic tiles in patterns like this one
Above right: The natural warmth of polished timber floors enhances any room setting

## Coir, seagrass and sisal matting

Tough, grassy fibres wear well, have great texture and lovely natural colours. They're do-it-yourself favourites but moisture can cause mildew, rotting and unpleasant odours. Matting should last around ten years with regular cleaning to prevent fibre damage from built-up grit and sand in the matting.

Lifestyle

## Cork tiles

A relatively short-term option for kitchens and playrooms, cork cushions tired feet and once sealed is easily cleaned with a moist, soft mop. Cork is less durable than vinyl and is generally only good for one 'recut' (resand) and reseal before needing replacement.

## Rubber tiles

Brightly coloured, high-tech tiles that are easy to lay and cut into patterns. Noise-absorbing, they are ideal for playrooms, kitchens and other high traffic areas. Rubber is non-slip and impervious to moisture. It's kind to tired legs and easy to clean.

## Terracotta tiles

Richly coloured, clay-based terracotta is an attractive choice and a sound investment, requiring little maintenance after sealing: just clean with a soft mop and a few drops of white vinegar in water. See the caution about early sealing of slate floors – the same applies to tiles. Do take care when working with tools or moving furniture as a dropped hammer or other heavy object can damage any highly glazed floor tile.

## Wood

Timber floors are beautiful and, once sealed, they are easy to clean, very durable and can be left unadorned or strewn with rugs. Timber strip floors are constructed from either hardwood (wears forever and comes in striking natural colours with little grain) or softwood (less durable but features lovely grain and knots, best for light traffic areas). Noise-absorbing parquet flooring panels are easy to lay and ideal for kitchens or family rooms. They wear quickly in high traffic areas and may need recutting and resealing about once every three years. Sweep timber floors with a soft broom and never use detergents or solvents on them. A few drops of fabric conditioner in a bucket of warm water, applied with a soft, moist (not wet) mop, can give a lovely finish.

## Vinyl

Choose either tiles or sheets (in different widths) in a multitude of colours and patterns, including superb slate or marble look-alikes. Vinyl tiles are thinner and more brittle than sheets but are easier to fit around difficult angles, and errors are less expensive because you only damage one or two tiles rather than a whole sheet. Their coarse finish scratches easily, recovers slowly from dents and needs more maintenance: not a good choice for busy rooms. Vinyl sheets are denser and more resilient: they recover faster from furniture and heel impressions. Some sheets feature cushion backing while some have a built-in sealant. Sheeting is more pliable than tiles and easier on the legs in kitchens and playrooms.

# Laying a Vinyl Tile Floor

*Vinyl tiles are an excellent surface for kitchen floors, easier to lay than sheet vinyl and easier to repair by replacing individual tiles.*

## Before You Begin

❏  To do the job properly it is essential that the floor underneath is perfectly flat, achievable only with concrete slabs that have been steel-trowelled or finished with self-levelling cement, or with rougher slabs and floorboards that have been covered with underlay sheets. This second option is more accessible to DIY enthusiasts.

❏  Underlay sheets are most likely to be of either masonite or fibre-cement, the latter being easier to lay, immune to water damage and giving a better, more rigid surface.

❏  Floor boards must be flat. If boards are badly warped the whole floor must be rough-sanded before the underlay can be fixed. Floor sanders can be hired and are worth the expense. Remove lumps from concrete with a cold chisel.

**Note:** Manufacturers supply information sheets that cover all aspects of this kind of job.

❏  When setting out the tiles, try to avoid tile edges falling within 80 mm of underlay joins. Avoid narrow pieces near walls and always use the cut edge against walls or cupboards rather than against other tiles.

❏  Use only the adhesive recommended by the tile manufacturer and follow instructions carefully.

❏  Use tiles laid loose to establish the longest perpendicular line through the room that will give an equal distance to the closest walls on either side. Use a chalk line, or a tight string line suspended between two nails.

MATERIALS
- ☐ tiles
- ☐ suitable adhesive
- ☐ underlay sheets
- ☐ nails

SPECIAL TOOLS NEEDED
- ☐ knife
- ☐ hammer
- ☐ notched trowel
- ☐ string or chalk
- ☐ disposable cloth
- ☐ steel ruler
- ☐ tape measure

METHOD

1  Start laying the underlay sheets in a corner of the room, keeping sheet edges about 3 mm away from the walls. Lay out all the sheets on the floor and cut where necessary before fixing any to the floor.

Fig.1

Gap

Gap

Half gap

Nail

Centre line

Nail

Fig.2
Wall
Tile to be cut
Gauge

2 Nail the sheets in place, ensuring that nail heads are flush with the surface of the sheets before laying the tiles. It may be necessary to sand the joints between the sheets if the floor beneath is really rough.

3 Sweep the floor carefully. Loose-lay tiles along and out from the centre line (see Fig.1), establishing what size the border tiles will be. Any one of these centre tiles can be laid first.

4 Using a notched trowel to spread the adhesive, prepare an area equal to about six tiles along the centre line. Place the tiles as close to their proper position as possible to avoid having to slide them. As each tile is laid, press it down with the palm of your hand and rub the surface firmly. You must assume that the tiles are cut perfectly square during manufacture so you should not allow any cracks to appear between them as they are laid. Immediately remove any adhesive which has spread on the floor or smeared the tiles.

**Note:** Boxes of tiles should be well-mixed before the first one is laid because you cannot assume that the colour will be constant from box to box. Selecting boxes with the same batch number when purchasing tiles gives some insurance.

5 When cutting tiles around the edges, lay the tile to be cut over the adjacent tile, making sure the pattern is the right way up. Then lay another full tile over the top and push it hard against the wall. You will now have a thickness of three tiles. Using the top tile as a gauge, score the second tile with your trimming knife (see Fig. 2). Remove the top tile and cut through the second tile and it will fit perfectly into the space. Repeat this process until all edge tiles are in place.

6 Walk around for a while on the tiles or hire a roller, making sure that all adhesive is removed and that all tiles are sticking down well. Wait 24 hours before moving heavy items, such as the fridge, into place on your new floor.

*Left: Easy-to-lay tiles make a great surface for kitchen floors*

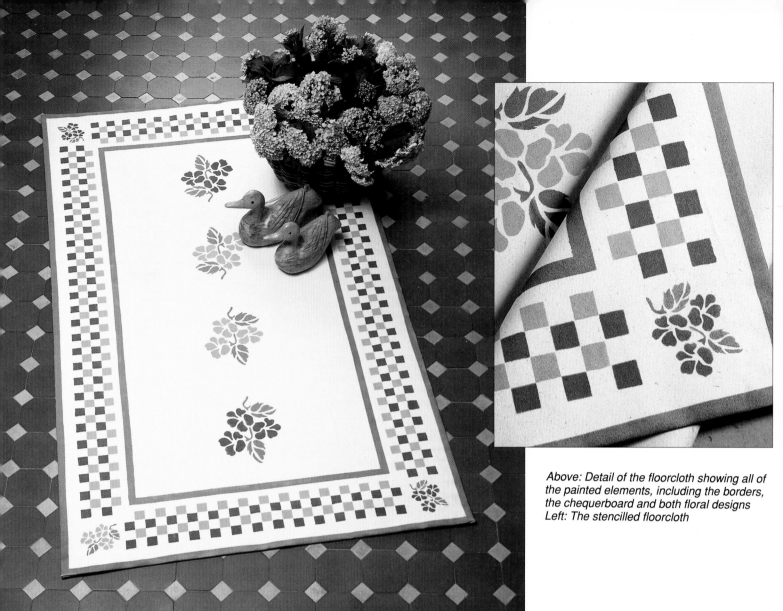

Above: Detail of the floorcloth showing all of the painted elements, including the borders, the chequerboard and both floral designs
Left: The stencilled floorcloth

# Stencilled Floorcloth

*Painted or stencilled floorcloths were popular in the 18th and 19th centuries as a cheap and colourful way to decorate the floors. Traditionally made of canvas and painted with housepaint, the cloths had a brittle surface which had a tendency to crack and discolour over a period of time. The availability of modern, fast-drying acrylic paints, and even specialised fabric inks, makes floorcloth decoration easier and gives greater durability.*

## Before You Begin

❏ When choosing your paints, it is advisable to use opaque inks, especially when printing onto a dark background.

❏ We recommend you make two chequerboard stencils because of the amount of stencilling to be done. The inks tend to build up on the stencils during use, thus reducing the size of the design.

❏ For small areas, use either a small stencil brush or even a cotton bud.

❏ You can cut separate stencils for each part of the design or mask off areas to be painted in a different colour with masking tape if using a single stencil.

❏ Primed artists' canvas can be used and does not need undercoat.

❏ Planning on graph paper helps with dimensions and corner placement.

❏ The background or undercoat for this floorcloth uses a transparent base for opaque screen printing inks (available through screen printing suppliers) but matt acrylic varnish or PVA adhesive glue (1 part glue : 5 parts water) can also be used.

## MATERIALS

The materials and measurements given here will make a floorcloth with finished measurements of 160 cm x 1 m.

**For the floorcloth:**
☐ 1.5 m of 180 cm wide heavy cotton canvas
☐ screen printing inks or acrylic paints in your choice of colours

56

- matt varnish (polyurethane) to seal the finished surface
- contact adhesive
- coloured pencils in the same colours as your paints
- 1.5 cm wide masking tape

## For the stencil:

- one 11.5 cm square manila card for the corner flower design; one 22 cm square manila card for the centre flower design; two 20 cm x 40 cm manila cards for the chequerboard design
- linseed oil
- turps (white spirit)
- fine lead pencil
- eraser for removing pencil markings
- stencil brushes (small and medium-sized) or sponges
- craft knife or sharp blade
- board or piece of glass on which to cut stencils

## METHOD

See Pull Out Pattern Sheet at the back of the book for the small floral and the chequerboard stencils. See page 103 for the large floral stencil.

### For the stencils:

**1** Draw two diagonal lines from corner to corner on each of the four blank pieces of manila card. The intersection of these lines indicates the centre of each manila card.

**2** Coat both sides of each manila card generously with a 50:50 mixture of linseed oil and mineral turpentine (white spirit) and allow to dry. Remove any excess oiliness by wiping with a soft cloth.

**3** To trace the stencil designs onto your oiled manila cards, position the corner flower design in the centre of the 11.5 cm square card and the centre flower design in the centre of the 22 cm square and trace.

**4** Draw a grid of 2.5 cm squares on the other two pieces of card, leaving a 5 cm border all around the edge of each card. Try to keep the chequerboard measurements as accurate as possible. Cut out alternate squares of the chequerboard pattern. At the 5 cm border line, cut a notch in each edge of the stencil cards, as shown on the Pattern Sheet. These notches will help you align the chequerboard pattern.

### For the floorcloth:

**1** Cut the sheet of canvas to measure 180 cm x 120 cm. This includes hem allowances of 10 cm.

**2** Lay the canvas out on a large flat surface, and weight or tack down the edges. Measure in 10 cm from each side and draw a fine pencil line. This is your hem marking.

**3** Place masking tape *outside* this rectangle with your tape edge along the pencil line. Using your undercoat or background colour, paint the canvas inside this taped rectangle and allow it to dry.

**4** Place a second piece of tape butting up against the inside edge of the first row of tape. Place a third row of tape, butting its edge up to the inside edge of the second. Remove the middle row of tape and put it aside for later use. This process will give you the correct size and location for painting the perimeter stripe. Cut away the tape overlap at the corners to give an uninterrupted border line.

**5** With green paint/ink, paint the stripe between the rows of masking tape. Allow to dry. Before removing the masking tape, trace around the inside edges with a fine pencil line. This will be where you will begin your chequerboard pattern.

**6** Position your 11.5 cm square piece of manila card in a corner with two sides of the card butted up against the inside edge of the masking tape. Trace around the outside of the card with a fine pencil line and repeat this procedure in each corner. This area will be used for stencilling the corner flower design.

**7** Position your chequerboard design with the notches in the short side edges aligned along the fine pencil line. Using a coloured pencil to match colour 1, trace around the inside of your stencil in the areas where you wish to use that colour. Position the stencil for colour 2 and, using an appropriately coloured pencil, repeat the procedure.

**8** Place the first chequerboard stencil back on the canvas, with the coloured lines as your guide and using a stencil brush or sponge, apply the appropriate colour with a dabbing motion. Allow the paint to dry and repeat the process using the second chequerboard stencil and the second colour.

**9** When the chequerboard pattern is dry, position the corner flower stencils, matching the edges of the card to the edges of the chequerboard pattern. Paint in the first colour. Place the same stencil in the diagonally opposite corner and paint in the same colour. Paint the second colour in the other corners.

**10** Position three rows of masking tape as before, this time *inside* the edge of the chequerboard design. Once again, remove the centre row of tape, and paint the green stripe as before.

### Centre design

To make a placement line for the central flower stencil, draw a line lengthways, down the centre of the floorcloth. Place the larger flower design stencil diagonally on this line, with the stem towards the centre and as close as possible to the inner border pattern. Place a small mark on the cloth where one corner of the card is nearest the centre. This is important, as it shows you where to position the card for the next flower, which is one step closer to the centre. Apply the paint with a light dabbing motion. Repeat this procedure, starting from the opposite end. You should then have four flower motifs along the centre line, with their stems all pointing towards the centre.

If you prefer to cluster the flowers in the centre, draw two centre guidelines, one lengthways and the other across the width. Simply place the stencil in each quarter with the stem towards the centre.

### To complete:

**1** When all the stencilling is completed and the ink is dry, carefully iron the floorcloth with a hot, *dry* iron. You must either iron the floorcloth on the wrong side or use a pressing cloth.

**2** Fold under the hem allowances and glue them in place, mitring corners. Place something heavy on the glued edges to ensure a good bond while it is drying.

**3** Coat the right side of the floorcloth with two or three coats of clear lacquer (acrylic or polyurethane) to protect and seal. If you are planning to store your floorcloth, it is best rolled not folded.

# Floor Finishes
**FEATURE**

If your floors are looking a bit sad and worn, don't decide immediately on covering them with fitted carpets. Often the solution to unattractive floors is a creative one, rather than a bank-breaking exercise!

Whichever method you choose, you will first need to fill all the knot holes with a proprietary wood filler and seal the finished, treated floor boards with clear polyurethane paint.

## Bleaching

Bleaching will result in a much lighter floor colour that can be sealed with polyurethane paint. The method is most suitable for floors that have not been stained, as stain soaks into the fibres of the timber and is difficult to eliminate completely although bleaching can lighten an existing stain. If the timber has been treated with stain and a polyurethane sealer in the past, it must be first sanded back to the stained timber.

Ensure good ventilation while you're working, as the fumes from bleach can be irritating.

### METHOD

1 Paint the floor with liquid bleach and allow it to soak into the timber. Continue to coat the floor with bleach until the desired lightness is achieved. This may be a slow process. After bleaching, wash the floor down with a 50:50 solution of white vinegar and water to neutralise the bleach. If the timber swells during bleaching, it is easily overcome with light sanding.

2 Seal with clear polyurethane paint following the maker's instructions.

## Staining

Staining does not have to be restricted to the traditional wood shades – you can be quite adventurous with your colour choices!

### METHOD

1 Select the stain colour of your choice. If the floor is new, or has been freshly sanded, apply the colour as the manufacturer directs.

2 If you have an existing stained and sealed floor, you will need to sand the floor back to a raw state, then proceed to stain with a new colour as the stain maker directs.

*Floor finishes from left to right: Bleached; limed and stencilled; stained and stencilled; limed; stained*

**3** Once you are satisfied with the colour achieved, seal the floor with clear polyurethane paint following maker's instructions.

## Stencilling

This decorative method of painting floors has stood the test of time! Creative people have long painted their floors, not only to save money, but to be able to enjoy a continuation of the design theme in their room. So often the floor is regarded only as a platform for the room, when it could be a decorative feature in its own right. Stencilling can be done over a previously stained and sealed floor.

Borders work very well on floors, especially as a frame for feature rugs. They can emphasise areas of the room, by giving visual definition to various sections, such as around fireplaces.

METHOD

**1** Sand back the surface of the floor where the paint is to be applied sufficiently to give a rough feel. This roughness will allow the stencil paint to adhere to the floor without the risk of it flaking off.

**2** Following our directions for **Stencilling a Border** on page 43, mark out where your decorated areas will be. When you are happy with the placement, draw in your guidelines and stencil in the designs.

**3** When the stencilled areas are completely dry, seal with clear polyurethane paint following the maker's instructions.

## Painted floors

This method of revamping a floor works very well in low-traffic areas, or in rooms that have a large central area covered by a rug. You can paint high-traffic areas, but you must be prepared for the paint to wear away quickly in these areas. You may

choose to paint with acrylic paints, wiping off the paint shortly after application in the direction of the grain using a lint-free cloth.

METHOD

**1** Paint can be applied over existing stain and sealer, but you will need to sand back any obvious rough areas before starting to paint.

**2** Be sure that you don't fall into the trap of painting yourself into a corner! Start painting at the furthest corner from the door, and work back towards the door.

**3** Making certain that the floor is dust-free, paint the floor with several coats of oil-based paint. Sanding back lightly between coats of paint will encourage the better adherence of subsequent coats of paint.

**4** Finally, seal the floor with one or two coats of clear polyurethane paint, following the maker's instructions.

# Seating
## *arrangements*

*W*ell, *you've papered the walls, chosen your floor coverings and now it's time to look at your furnishings. New living room furniture can be very costly, so investigate what alternatives are available. Big floor cushions are probably the most economical solution to the seating problem, though not necessarily the most comfortable. They are quite simple to make and you can discard them later as you replace them with more substantial pieces.*

*If you already have a sofa which is looking a bit 'tired', consider having it recovered or, better still, doing the job yourself. Do-it-yourself upholstery requires a lot of patience and some specific skills. Check out your local community college or night classes for a suitable course, or the local library for a book with good step-by-step directions. If this still sounds a bit out of your league, then our convertible sofa bed is the perfect answer to your problem. No special skills are necessary, just some readily available raw materials and your sewing machine.*

Fully upholstered armchair

Wing sofa

Chair with pad seat

Ottoman with attached cushion

# Cover Stories
### FEATURE

Wouldn't that old sofa that you bought at the last church jumble sale look great with a smart new cover? A few metres of fabric and a couple of weekends' work and ...hey presto, a new sofa! If only it were that easy.

Traditional furniture upholstery can be a mine of pitfalls for the amateur. Furnishing fabrics are expensive and mistakes can quickly swallow up your budget. Even the simplest type of upholstery involves fixing a covering fabric over a tightly stretched calico which itself covers padding of some kind and possibly the addition of springs.

The variety of furniture shapes and styles is almost endless. There are fully upholstered pieces – some with wooden arms, some with exposed timber frames, some with loose cushions, others with fixed cushions, or any combination of these. Some furniture pieces have shapes which create particular problems and awkward corners to work around.

Upholstery is a distinct craft, requiring special skills, knowledge, materials and tools. For a traditional upholstery project, a professional upholsterer is usually the best choice. However, if you are really interested in learning the craft, find out what courses are available in your local community.

Investing a little time learning the tricks of the trade will save you much time and trouble. You will find out the best materials to use, what tools are needed and where to buy them; and, most importantly, you'll have ongoing instruction and support as you work your way through a project. There are, of course, very simple cover projects – such as renewing dining room chairs, or re-covering cushions – that you can do. These projects are not 'upholstery' in the traditional sense – no repairs or new stuffing, webbing or springs are required.

## Fabric fantasies

Decorating with fabric is a bit like painting a beautiful picture in your room. Instead of mixing colours on a canvas you create the effect you want with the colours and patterns of your fabrics. When it comes down to it, no-one but you will know

Two-deck-cushion sofa

Barrel-back chair

Ottoman with attached cushion

about the hours you spent replacing the 'insides' of your chair, but they will certainly notice the colour and style of the covers you have chosen.

Choosing the right fabric for the job and the room is crucial to a successful project, but the great variety of fabrics available can be daunting for the home decorator. The four natural fibres – cotton, wool, silk and linen – are all widely used in home furnishings:
❑ Cotton, which is mass produced and generally economical, is a popular choice for curtains, slipcovers and cushions.
❑ Wool is very hard-wearing, flame resistant, light and relatively waterproof. It is popular for furniture coverings.
❑ Silk is the glamour fabric but because of its relatively high cost is usually reserved for trimming, cushions or luxury pieces.
❑ Linen is one of the world's

oldest domestic fibres and because of its long-wearing qualities has always been a popular choice for home furnishings.

Many man-made or synthetic fibres are also available these days and are often blended with natural fibres. This reduces the fabric cost as well as taking advantage of the good wearing and washing qualities of polyester and viscose.

## Colour and pattern

The choice of colour and pattern for a particular covering project will be determined by a number of factors. Are you decorating a whole room or will your new cover have to fit in with existing pieces? Is your room big enough to cope with that large splashy floral or will it be overwhelmed? Do you already have a strong pattern in that room? Do you

need to warm up a room with yellows, pinks and reds or do you need to cool it down with a blue or mauve?

Remember that colours can be affected by the light in a room, both natural and artificial. Before buying metres of fabric, take home a sample piece, drape it over your sofa or chair and leave it there for a day or two. Then you can judge the effect of the light in the room and how you think it will fit in with curtains, wallpaper and other colours and patterns in the room. Generally the larger your room the more you can get away with in colour and pattern. There are exceptions, of course, but as a rule of thumb, it will help you to avoid decorating disasters.

Matching patterns where fabric pieces join can be a nightmare. If you are not experienced, or endowed with the patience of

Job, you are probably best to stick to plains or all-over small prints, which do not need matching. Stripes do need careful matching but provide their own easy-to-follow guidelines. Florals or medallion patterns are more difficult because the motif has to be centred on seats and backs, wasting a lot of fabric. Checks are the hardest of all, having to be matched in all directions at once. Check before you buy whether the fabric you like will present matching problems. Lay two lengths side by side as though they were joined, then move one slightly up or down. Now stand back and see the difference. You can do the same test if patterns are to meet 'end-to-end' or 'side-to-end'.

**Golden rules for choosing fabric:**

❏ Be sure that the fabric you choose is suitable for the job you are doing. Don't let your enthusiasm cloud your judgement.

❏ Be sure your purchase is economically sound. Don't overspend on areas that don't warrant it but do buy the best you can afford, especially for high-use areas. If you have fallen for an incredibly expensive cushion fabric that you really can't afford, perhaps you could use just a little of it as a feature and team it with a less expensive background fabric.

❏ If you are going to sew soft furnishings at home, be sure that your sewing machine is up to the job. Remember, you may have to sew through four and five layers of fabric.

❏ Make sure you check on wearability, stretch and colourfastness before you buy. Generally the tighter the weave, the less the fabric is likely to stretch out of shape.

# Fabric Know-How
## FEATURE

Whether it's inexpensive cotton used extravagantly, patchwork quilts, lush silk drapes or antique tapestries born again as small cushions, fabrics make a statement about you and generally set the decorating theme.

You don't have to spend a lot of money – often it's the creative use of inexpensive fabrics that is the most effective. Remember, whether you're considering furniture or fabrics, good design doesn't have to cost any more than poor design.

The great variety of fabrics available to choose from can be daunting to the fledgling home decorator. Apart from traditional knowledge about fabrics and their properties, manufacturers today often have helpful information printed on the sample cards, telling you of a fabric's washing abilities and its potential for fading. They will refer to the 'wearability' of the fabric – or in other words, how strong it is! Pay attention to this valuable information. Fabrics are only guaranteed by the manufacturer if used in recommended situations.

The four natural fibres, cotton, wool, silk and linen are all familiar in home furnishing. Cotton has long been the leader for sheets, towels and most curtains. It's mass produced and this helps to make it inexpensive to manufacture into fabrics of many weights and textures. Wool is the basis of traditional and modern floor coverings. Wool is the best fabric insulator while being hard wearing, flame retardant, light and fairly waterproof. It is long-

lasting, but take care with laundering. Silk has the glamour role, providing traditional fabrics for upholstery, tassels and braids, cushions and luxury rugs. Silk is a very fine and strong fibre, a good insulator, quite expensive compared to other natural fibres, and is the most lustrous fibre of all. Linen is the world's oldest domestic fibre. Sheets and household napery have always been made from linen, with its main appeal being its sheer endurance – it never seems to wear out!

Today you still have the choice of natural fibres, but also have access to the wide range of man-made or synthetic fibres. The most commonly used of these fibres are polyester, acrylic and viscose – all produced by chemical processes and all with valuable qualities.

Synthetic fibres are often blended with man-made fibres in fabrics. This serves two purposes – the cost is reduced, and very often the synthetic fibres give added strength. Synthetic fabrics usually wash very well, the fibres do not absorb dirt and moisture, and are long wearing. They also provide insulation and effective light control.

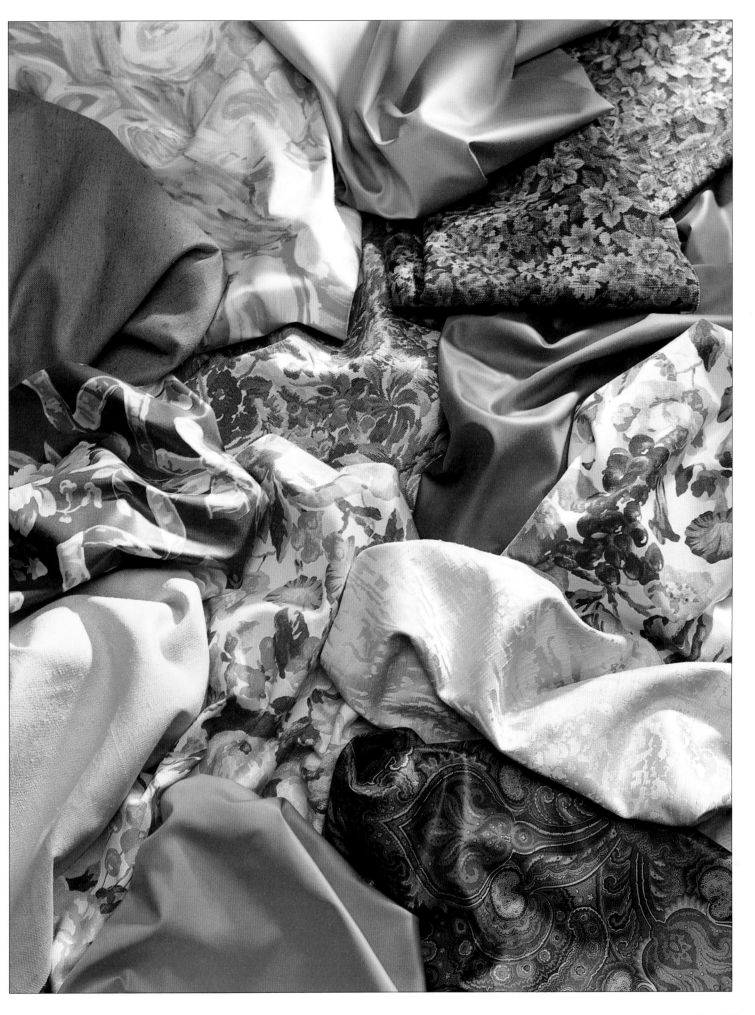

# Slipcover Set

*This easy-cover project may be the perfect opportunity to convert six odd chairs into a matched set!*

## Before You Begin

❏ This slipcover pattern is designed for chairs which are flush across the top of the backrest with no protruding knobs – all the lines and surfaces of the chair should be as straight as possible. Bowed backs and curved seats will not allow the fabric to hang properly.

❏ Choose your fabric carefully. You will need a sturdy material that doesn't present too many problems with matching patterns on adjacent surfaces. There is no set pattern because the dimensions of each chair are different.

*Below: Take advantage of the great range of fantasy fabrics available*
*Bottom left: Cutting and construction diagrams*

Laura Ashley (Australia) Pty Limited

❏ You will need to take the measurements of your own chair to calculate the amount of fabric and the pattern pieces to cut. Measure the following:

*Length x width of chair* – the length from the seat up the chair back and down to the floor (allowing for the width of the chair frame at the top of the backrest) by the width of the chair (allowing for the width of the chair frame at the sides). Cut one.

*Depth of seat x width of chair* – the depth of the seat plus the distance to the floor by the width of the chair. Cut one.

*Depth of seat x width of frame x height of seat from floor* – the depth of the seat plus the width of the timber frame by the height of the seat from the floor. Cut two.

Once you have established these measurements you can calculate the amount of fabric required.

❏ Choose a contrasting or complementary fabric for the lining as it is sure to show at the joins. If you like, the slipcover can be lined with the main fabric for an all-over look.

❏ For added comfort, include a layer of wadding between the main fabric and the lining.

## BEFORE

❏ Using your measurements, draw the pattern pieces onto suitable paper, brown wrapping paper is a good choice, marking in significant points.

### MATERIALS
☐ sufficient fabric and lining (see *Before You Begin*)
☐ matching sewing thread
☐ fabric or ribbon for ties

### METHOD

**1** Cut out the pattern pieces from main and lining fabric, allowing 1.5 cm all round for seams. Take care to match and centre any fabric pattern at this point.

**2** Sew side extensions in place, attaching them at the top and sides of the backrest (Fig.1). Sew back to seat and front (Fig.2) then attach sides in place (Fig.3).

**3** Cut eight 30 cm lengths of ribbon or make ties out of cover fabric. Pin one end of each tie just below seat height on the front and back edges, keeping raw edges even.

**4** Make the lining in the same way as the cover. Place the lining and cover together with right sides facing. Sew around the outside, leaving an opening for turning and catching the ties as you sew. Turn the cover right side out, taking care to push the corners out completely. Press.

**AFTER**

*Top: This easy-cover project has transformed a plain dining chair (Top left)*
*Right: Detail of side split and tie*

# Sofa Bed and Pillows

*In the wink of an eye, this very clever sofa changes into a double bed for those unexpected guests. It would look just as good covered in a geometric print, denim or traditional mattress ticking.*

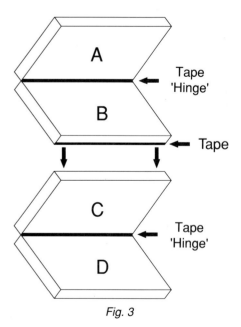

## Before You Begin

❏ The size of your sofa bed is pretty much up to you. We have used a double-bed size piece of foam, cut into four pieces. You may prefer to buy the four pieces already cut, if these are available.

❏ We have used foam that is approximately 15 cm thick. If your foam is a different thickness, adjust your fabric measurements accordingly.

### MATERIALS

☐ piece of foam approximately 137 cm x 183 cm x 15 cm thick
☐ 7 m of 180 cm wide plain desuti, light-weight canvas, denim or heavy calico
☐ 5 m of 4 cm wide firm, cotton webbing tape or twill tape
☐ 2 pillows
☐ one double bed feather or polyester-filled continental quilt
☐ 12 mm wide coloured cotton tape, enough to stitch around the outside edges of the quilt and down each channel and around the pillowcases. One side of an average double quilt will use about 35 m

### METHOD

1.5 cm seams allowed throughout.

**1** Measure the foam and mark crossways cutting lines to divide it into four equal blocks – each approximately 137 cm x 46.5 cm x 15 cm. To cut foam, it is best to use an electric carving knife or jigsaw and to raise the foam up on house bricks.

**2** Make paper patterns of the sides, ends, top and bottom surfaces. Add

1.5 cm seam allowances all around each piece. Cut 8 side panels, 8 end panels, 8 top/bottom panels. Cut 2 pillowcases, each 175 cm x 50 cm.

**3** Mark each one of the four foam blocks A, B, C and D.

#### To cover blocks A and D:

**1** Take two side pieces and two end pieces and join the short ends together to form a strip then join the ends to form an open rectangular box. (See Fig. 1)

**2** On the right side of the fabric, sew a length of webbing tape to one long edge of one side piece, starting and ending 1.5 cm from both corner seams, with the tape lapping over the edge of the fabric by about 2 cm. (See Fig. 1)

**3** Pin the top panel to the box, matching corners to seams and stitch all around. Pin the bottom panel to the other side of the box and sew on three sides – leaving the taped side open. (See Fig. 2)

#### To cover block B:

**1** Join side and end panels as for A and D (see Fig. 1). Sew one length of webbing tape to one long side panel as for A and D.

**2** Take a top edge of the opposite long panel and stitch it to the webbing protruding from block A, still leaving the seam open. Attach the top and bottom panels, still leaving the taped edge open. Turn the cover right side out.

#### To cover block C:

**1** Join side and end panels into an open box as for B but do not sew on any tape. Stitch top and bottom panels to sides, leaving open one top edge and one

diagonally opposite bottom edge of the long side panels. Join to cushion D in the same way as A and B. Turn CD right side out. This gives you two hinged pairs AB and CD. (See Fig. 3)

**2** Handstitch the AB pair of cushions to the CD pair, by inserting the tape from B into the still-open seam in C, so that they will fold in an M or W shape when viewed from the end. (See Fig. 4)

*Fig. 1*

*Fig. 2*

*Fig. 3*

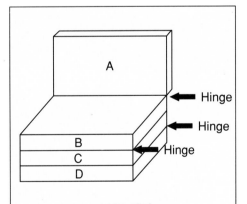

Fig. 4

*Above Left: The cushions are folded to form the sofa and covered with the trimmed quilt*

*Above: Opened out, the sofa is now a comfortable bed*

**3** Ease the foam blocks inside the covers at the hinged openings. Fold under each opening seam allowance and slipstitch it to the tape, so that the cover fits snugly and the connecting seam is closed.

**4** Placed about 10 cm from the wall, the top cushion flips up to form the back of the sofa and converts easily to a double bed.

**For the pillowcases:**

**1** Turn under 6 mm on the short ends of the fabric. Turn under another 1 cm. Stitch down and press. Fold 5 cm under on one end. Stitch in place. Fold 15 cm under on the other end. Pin side seams. Match the two ends together and press. Remove pins.

**2** Measure 12 cm from both folds and top and bottom edges. Mark these lines with dressmaker's chalk. Pin col-oured tape around the rectangles as marked. Stitch tape into place, mitring its corners as you go. You will have a border of tape on both sides of the pillowcase.

**3** Fold the trimmed pillowcase as shown on page 105 with right sides facing. Stitch sides. Take care to secure the stitching well at the open end. Turn to right side and press.

## Throwover quilt

We have decorated an inexpensive, purchased quilt for use with the sofa bed. During the day it provides an attractive cover and at night can be slipped into a single bed quilt cover. Stitch coloured tape around all the edges and down the channels of the quilt. You can stitch this on one side only or on both, as you prefer.

### HINT

An easy way to see how the sofa hinges, is to tape together four empty audio cassette cases, marked A, B, C and D, according to the diagrams. You will find it helpful to refer to this while you are making the sofa.

# Director's Chair Cover

*The director's chair has found a place in many households at one time or another. Reasonably priced, comfortable and easy to store, it can undergo endless transformations. This is a great way to dress up a director's chair. Whether you choose a plain fabric such as ours or a bold print, these inexpensive chairs will take on a whole new look.*

# Stencilled Director's Chair

## Before You Begin

❑ Remove the existing covers from your chair and use them to estimate the fabric for new covers. Don't forget to leave seam and hem allowances. It is sometimes possible to buy replacement covers for director's chairs, ready for decorating. Before you buy, check that they will fit.

❑ The manila card for making your stencils is generally available from stationery suppliers. You can, of course, use firm plastic sheets if you prefer.

MATERIALS

☐ sufficient fabric, such as a lightweight canvas
☐ screen printing inks
☐ stencil brushes or sponges (1 for each colour)
☐ two pieces of manila card, one 11.5 cm square for the flower motif and one 22 cm x 40 cm for the chequerboard
☐ mineral turpentine (white spirit)
☐ linseed oil
☐ craft knife or sharp blade
☐ board or sheet of glass for cutting stencil on
☐ eraser
☐ coloured pencils (as close as possible to the colours you are using)
☐ fine lead pencil

METHOD

See Pull Out Pattern Sheet at the back of the book for the stencil patterns.

1 Using the old covers as your pattern, cut new back and seat covers for the chair. Finish the edges, with overlocking, zigzag stitching or as you prefer, to prevent fraying, and mark the hem turnings. Do not sew the seams at this stage.

### For the chequerboard stencil:

1 Mix mineral turpentine (white spirit) and linseed oil to 50:50 proportions. Apply fairly generously to both sides of the 22 cm x 40 cm manila card. Allow to dry. Remove excess oiliness with a soft cloth.

2 Draw a 2.5 cm squared grid on the card, leaving a 5 cm wide border all around the edge. Keep the chequerboard measurements as accurate as possible.

Cut a notch at the edges of the card where the 5 cm border lines meet the edges. These notches will be your placement guides.

3 Cut out alternate squares on the first line. Leave the second line. Cut the third line as for the first. Continue in this way until you reach the opposite border.

4 Measure 2.5 cm from each hem marking and draw a fine vertical pencil line. This will be the placement line for the edge of your stencil design.

5 Position your stencil on the fabric so that the notches are aligned along your pencil line. Using a coloured pencil in your first colour, trace around the inside of the stencil in the areas where you wish to use that colour.

6 Reposition the stencil for your second colour and repeat the above step, using the second colour pencil.

7 Position the stencil on the fabric, using the coloured lines as a guide. Paint in the first colour. Allow it to dry before stencilling with the second colour.

### For the floral stencil:

1 Using the floral stencil on the pattern sheet, or your own design if you prefer, stencil the chair back panel. You can place the design any way you want, repeating the design on the chair seat also if you wish.

2 Prepare the 11.5 cm square stencil card in the same way as for the chequerboard stencil. Draw two diagonal pencil lines, connecting opposite corners of the card. This marks the centre of your stencil. Trace your design onto the centre of the card. Cut out the stencil. Using coloured pencils in the same colours as the paints you have chosen, draw around the elements of the stencil design.

3 Paint your design with a dabbing motion, completing one colour and allowing it to dry before painting with the other one.

4 When the paint is dry, iron the covers on the wrong side with a hot dry iron for about four to five minutes. This will set the inks so that they can be washed without the risk of your design disappearing.

5 Pin the hems at the marked turnings and check the fit before sewing. Stitch the seams as marked. Replace the covers on your chair.

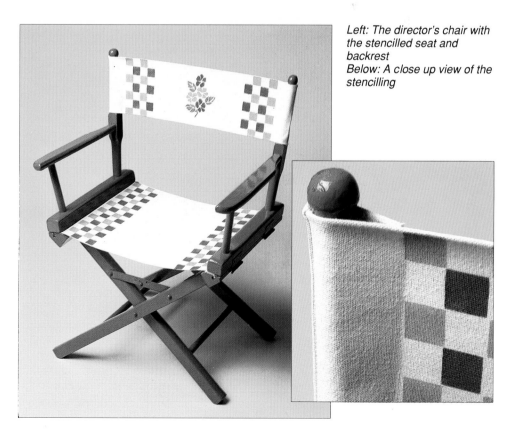

Left: The director's chair with the stencilled seat and backrest
Below: A close up view of the stencilling

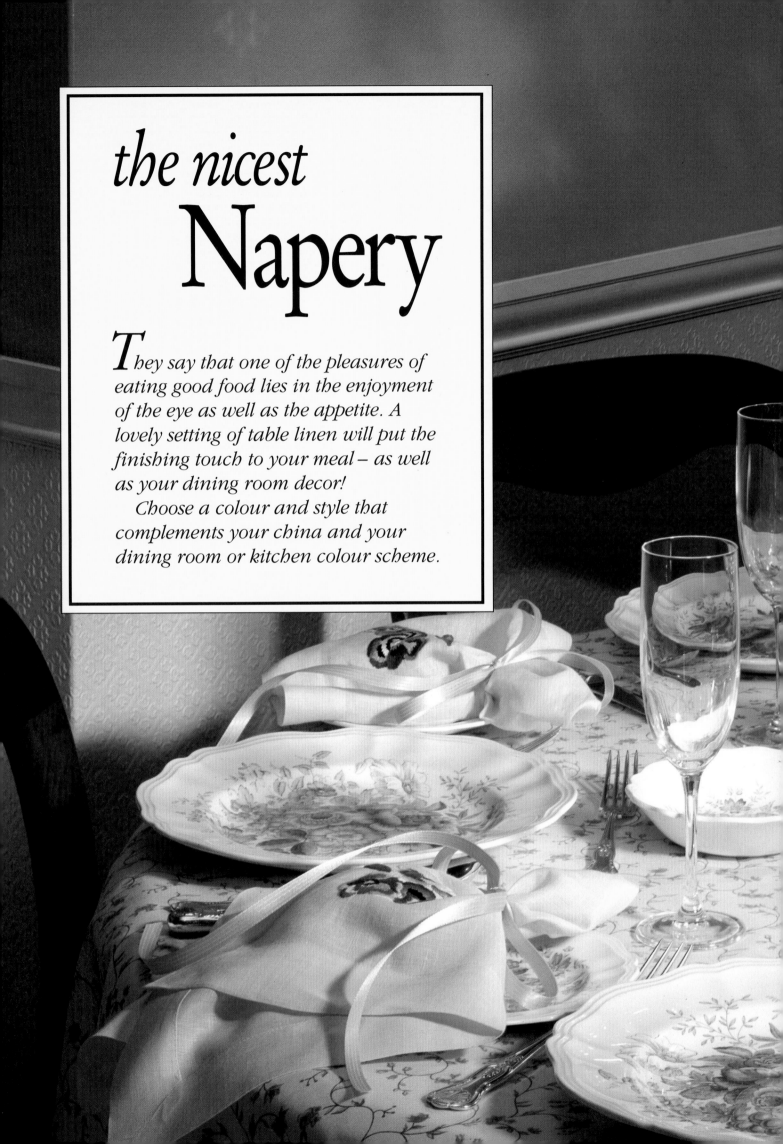

# the nicest
# Napery

*T*hey say that one of the pleasures of eating good food lies in the enjoyment of the eye as well as the appetite. A lovely setting of table linen will put the finishing touch to your meal – as well as your dining room decor!

Choose a colour and style that complements your china and your dining room or kitchen colour scheme.

# Stencilled Cloth and Napkins

## Before You Begin

❏ Measure your table to decide on the size of your cloth by running a tape measure across the table and over the sides to the depth you wish for the overhang. Be sure to include in your fabric allowance, the tabletop measurement and overhang for all four sides. Sometimes fabric can be so wide that you do not have to join pieces to reach the required size. If this width is not obtainable, join strips so that the seams run along near the table edges, rather than one seam down the middle of the table.

❏ It is best to choose a one hundred per cent cotton fabric with a smooth finish for a tablecloth and napkins. Cotton launders well and is pleasant to handle. If you prefer the wearing qualities of man-made fibres, try using a polyester/cotton mixture.

❏ There are many ways to locate the stencil design on your tablecloth, depending on the size of the cloth and the design, and your own preference. You could place the design at each place setting, as a continuous border around the edge of the cloth or positioned to sit in from the edge of the table, as in the one shown. Bear in mind when positioning your design, that the edge of the tablecloth is not likely to be visible when you are seated at the table so much of the effect could be lost.

## MATERIALS

### For the tablecloth:
☐ Allow sufficient fabric to cover table top and desired overhang, plus 5 cm all around for hem

### For each napkin:
☐ 60 cm square of fabric

### For both:
☐ matching sewing thread
☐ manila card for the stencil
☐ mineral turpentine (white spirit)
☐ linseed oil
☐ lead pencil
☐ sharp craft knife
☐ board for cutting stencil
☐ stencilling paints
☐ stencilling brushes
☐ masking tape

## METHOD

1 cm seams allowed throughout.

### For the tablecloth and napkins:

1 Fold the fabric as shown in the diagram below, having the edge 'A' measure 8 cm and the hems all 1 cm.

2 Stitch across the corners, trim seams. Turn the border to the right side.

3 Pin and baste inner edge in place. Stitch down and press.

### For the stencilling:

1 Mix mineral turpentine (white spirit) and linseed oil in a ratio of 50:50. Coat both sides of the manila card quite liberally with the mixture. Any excess oiliness can be wiped off with a soft cloth.

2 Draw the design onto the card. Cut out the stencil with a sharp craft knife.

3 Position the stencil on the cloth and napkins. Paint in first one colour and then any other colours one by one. Cover with masking tape any area that you wish to paint a different colour.

4 To set the colours, press on the wrong side of the fabric with a dry iron on a setting suitable for the fabric.

*Above: Folding and stitching diagram for mitred corners*
*Right: The linen cloth and napkins stencilled to match the china pattern*

# Primary Brights

*If you can sew straight, these place mats and napkins are just right for you. The skills involved are as simple as can be, and you will be delighted with the imaginative colour combinations possible. You could choose your own colours and even patterns to mix and match – black and white, pattern and plain, or simply crisscross the base with pretty braid.*

## Before You Begin

❏ One hundred per cent cotton fabric is ideal for making table linen. It washes well and is available in a wonderful array of colours. If you prefer a synthetic fabric for its wearing qualities, choose a cotton and polyester mixture for the best of both worlds.

## Place mat with coloured bands

### MATERIALS

**For each place mat:**

☐ piece of fabric 50 cm x 34 cm for the base
☐ polyester wadding 50 cm x 34 cm for the base
☐ piece of fabric for the contrast backing 56 cm x 40 cm
☐ five strips of contrast fabric each 34 cm x 4 cm
☐ three strips of contrast fabric each 50 cm x 4 cm
☐ matching sewing threads

### METHOD

1 cm seams allowed throughout.

**1** Baste fabric base to wadding around the edges and through the centre to hold the fabric smoothly in place.

**2** Fold in 6 mm on the long edges of each contrast fabric strip. Press. Using dressmaker's chalk, divide the base into 6 cm squares separated by 2 cm wide contrast bands and a 2 cm wide contrast border all around. Pin bands into place on base, weaving them over and under each other as shown. Stitch along both edges of each strip to secure in place.

**3** Place trimmed base onto the centre of the contrast backing piece with wrong sides facing. Baste together around the edge of the trimmed base. Note that the backing piece extends 3 cm beyond the trimmed piece on all sides. This extension will form the contrast border. Turn in 1 cm on all edges of backing piece. Mitre the contrast backing corners as shown on page 56, having A measure 4 cm.

**4** Fold extensions of the backing to the right side, enclosing the edges of trimmed piece. Stitch around the inner edge of the border, close to the fold and through all thicknesses.

*From left to right: Bound napkin; quilted and bound place mat; bound napkin; place mats with coloured bands and matching napkins*

# Napkins with contrast borders

## MATERIALS

**For each napkin:**
- ☐ 50 cm square of main fabric
- ☐ four 50 cm x 7 cm contrast fabric strips for borders
- ☐ matching sewing thread

## METHOD

1 cm seams allowed throughout.

**1** Cut the ends of the fabric strips to perfect diagonals. Fold in 1 cm on the inner (shorter) edge. Press.

**2** Seam the strips together at the corners to form an open square. Press the seams open.

**3** Place the right side of the contrast border square over wrong side of the main fabric piece, with raw edges matching. Stitch all around the outer edge. Trim the corners to reduce bulk. Turn the border to the right side and press. Stitch around the inner edge of border, through all thicknesses.

*Fig. 1*

# Quilted and bound place mat

## MATERIALS

- ☐ two pieces of main fabric, each 50 cm x 34 cm
- ☐ polyester wadding 50 cm x 34 cm
- ☐ 1.80 m of 4.2 cm wide bias binding, either purchased or cut from a contrast fabric
- ☐ matching sewing thread

## METHOD

1 cm seams allowed throughout.

**1** Place the wadding between the two main fabric pieces, so that the fabrics are right side out. Baste around the edges. Using a kitchen saucer as a guide, round off the corners.

**2** Using the photograph as a guide, divide the place mat into squares and mark with dressmaker's chalk. Stitch along the chalk rows to quilt.

**3** Position the bias on the wrong side of the place mat, with right sides facing and with your stitching line 1 cm in from the bias binding edge and 1.5 cm from the place mat edge. Stitch bias binding around the place mat, easing it around the curved corners and tucking the raw end under at the overlap. Press under 1 cm on the other raw end of the bias binding. Fold bias binding to the right side of the place mat. Pin then stitch along the folded edge. (See Fig. 1)

# Bound napkin

## MATERIALS

- ☐ 50 cm square of main fabric
- ☐ 1.10 m of 4.2 cm wide bias binding, purchased or cut from contrast fabric

## METHOD

**1** Using a kitchen saucer as a guide, round off the corners of the napkin.

**2** Bind the edges of the napkin following the directions for binding the place mat and using the diagram in Fig. 1.

# Pretty Pastels

*Create your own heirlooms! These place mats and napkins are sewn from lightweight pure linen – a timeless fabric that lasts and lasts.*

## Before You Begin

❏ All place mats and napkins, except B, are the same size and made in the same way. They differ only in the manner of trimming. The place mat and napkin B are trimmed first, then made following the BASIC SEWING METHOD.

### MATERIALS

**For each set:**
☐ piece of fabric 60 cm x 40 cm for the basic place mat
☐ piece 60 cm x 60 cm for basic napkin

**For set A:**
☐ embroidery thread

**For set B:**
☐ six different coloured sewing threads

**For set C:**
☐ a motif from a floral, cotton fabric
☐ matching sewing thread

**For set D:**
☐ silk braid or embroidery floss, suitable for hand-stitched couching
☐ matching sewing thread

**For set E:**
☐ embroidery floss in the appropriate colours for your design

### BASIC SEWING METHOD

1 cm seams allowed throughout.

**1** Mitre corners as shown on page 74, having A measure 7 cm.

**2** Fold the fabric as shown on page 74, pressing in hems and stitching lines. Stitch across corners, trim seam, turn to the right side. Press.

**3** Stitch around inner folded edge. Press carefully using a warm iron and damp cloth or ironing spray.

**For trimming set A:**
See the Pull Out Pattern Sheet at the back of the book for the place mat and napkin embroidery design.

**1** Trace the design onto one corner of the place mat and napkin. Embroider the outline using embroidery floss in your chosen colours and buttonhole stitch.(See Fig.1)

**2** When the embroidery is complete, carefully cut away the fabric inside the embroidered outline using small sharp scissors.

**For trimming set B:**

**1** Press a crease 5 cm in from all edges on both the place mat and the napkin. Using this crease as your starting and finishing point, stitch 6 rows of twin-needle stitching across the mat and napkin using six different colours (see picture below.) Be sure to stitch your corners so that the stitching remains on the right side.

*Fig. 1: Buttonhole stitch*

C

B

D

**2** When the stitching is complete, finish corners and borders following the BASIC SEWING METHOD given on page 78.

### For set C:

**1** Cut out a floral motif from a print fabric, allowing 6 mm fabric excess around motif.

**2** Position appliqué pieces on the place mat and napkin. Baste. Stitch around the edge of each piece, 6 mm from the edge using a small zigzag stitch. Cut away the excess fabric, close to the stitching. Adjust your sewing machine stitch to a wider satin stitch. Stitch again over the previous stitching, enclosing raw edge as you stitch. Do this for each appliqué piece, using matching sewing thread.

### For set D:

**1** The couching design is worked at random onto the place mat and napkin, forming a border around the centre. If you are using a sewing machine with a braiding foot attachment, follow the manufacturer's instructions for its use. If stitching by hand, use small, evenly spaced stitches. You may like to use a metallic embroidery thread for stitching.

**2** Lay the silk braid along the fabric, forming the curled design, and stitch over it, securing it to the fabric. (see below)

*Fig. 2: Couching*

### For set E:
See the Pull Out Pattern Sheet at the back of the book for the pansy design.

**1** Trace the pansy design from the Pattern Sheet on to the fabric, using dressmaker's tracing paper.

**2** Embroider the design as shown using long and short stitch (see Fig. 3) for the pansy petals and leaves and satin stitch for the centre of each flower as shown. (See Fig. 4)

*Fig. 3: Long and short stitch*

*Fig. 4: Satin stitch*

*From left to right: Place mat and napkin sets – Set C; set B; set D; set A; set E*

A

E

# Country
## *kitchen*

*T*raditionally, a country kitchen shines with the warm patina of polished timbers, slate or tile floors and an abundance of those small 'country' touches. These include wreaths of dried flowers; bowls of fruit and vegetables; collections of old china or cooking implements displayed on open shelves or in an old dresser; and a pot holder, curtains, place mats and so on, made from a pretty, small-print fabric.

You may not be in a position to scrap your existing kitchen and start again but you can add those clever details that will give your kitchen decor a country feel. Try your hand at the old craft of paper pricking and then apply it to your kitchen shelves. Sew our collection of fabric bits and pieces and don't forget the matching curtains. If your kitchen has suitable walls, adding an old-fashioned stencil border, such as the one on page 43, is a great finishing touch.

# Pierced or Pricked Paper

*This is one of the simplest crafts around and you don't need any glues, paints or special tools. You can use many types of paper, for example, writing papers, shelf trims, gift wrapping and even old greeting cards.*

## Before You Begin

❏ Use a firm type of paper but one that is not too rigid, as the indentations will be hard to make.

❏ This technique is also good for trimming writing paper. Large holes can sometimes be attractive in amongst a design, and these are created with the single-hole paper punch.

MATERIALS

☐ suitable paper
☐ a sharp darning needle or a noticeboard pin which has a portion of plastic at its base, for making the holes
☐ a sheet of soft particle board for resting the paper on
☐ dressmaker's pins to hold the paper and design sheet in place on the particle board
☐ a single-hole paper punch used to make the larger holes
☐ a design to use as a pattern

METHOD

**1** Place the paper onto the particle board. Position the decorative pattern over the paper. Secure the two layers together by pinning through the design in several places so that the hole you make becomes part of the design.

**2** Continue to pierce the paper, following the pattern. Make the indentations about 3 mm apart, and try to keep them evenly spaced.

*Above: Pricked paper shelf edging*
*Left: A country kitchen with all the trimmings*
*Below: Pricking diagram for the shelf edging*

## Decorative shelf papers

### Before You Begin

❏ You will need firm paper of a size which covers the shelf and allows the desired drop over the front of the shelf.

❏ You will have both raised 'bumps' and a flat surface resulting from the paper being pierced. Decide which side you wish to have as your right side. If you wish to have a combination of both you will need to flip the paper over and reposition the pattern while you work.

METHOD

**1** Place the design to be pierced just in from the edge of the paper, then continue, following the general instructions for paper pricking on this page.

**2** Cut the paper away to within 5-6 mm of the outside edge of the design to give the shelf paper an interesting edge.

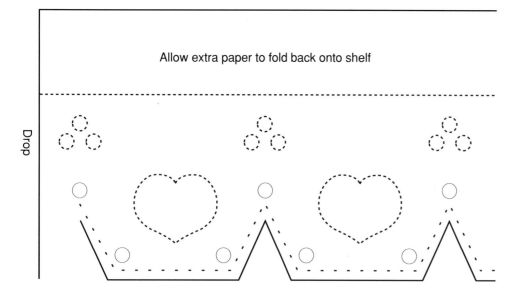

Allow extra paper to fold back onto shelf

Drop

# Quilted Kitchen Set

*You will see that all of these pieces use prequilted fabric, teamed with the matching unquilted material, or you can quilt your own fabric. To do this, baste a piece of polyester wadding to the wrong side of your plain fabric and stitch over it with a pattern of diagonal rows of stitches.*

## Pot holder

### MATERIALS

- ☐ two pieces of prequilted cotton main fabric, each 90 cm x 20 cm or plain fabric and polyester wadding in the same size
- ☐ two pieces 23 cm x 20 cm main fabric and two pieces of the same size from a contrasting cotton fabric for hand pieces
- ☐ 3 m of corded piping
- ☐ matching sewing thread

### METHOD

1 cm seams allowed throughout.

**1** Quilt fabric, if necessary, following the instructions on HOW TO QUILT FABRIC in the box on page 84.

**2** Sew corded piping to one 20 cm edge of each main fabric hand piece, with right sides facing and raw edges matching. Pin lining hand pieces over trimmed pieces, with right sides facing and raw edges matching. Stitch the 20 cm seam following previous stitching. Turn the hand pieces right sides out and press.

**3** Place the trimmed hand pieces at opposite ends of one main piece, with raw edges matching. Pin in place, then place remaining main piece on top of pinned main piece, so that raw edges are matching. Pin through all thicknesses. Using a kitchen cup as a guide, round off the corners of the pot holder. Remove untrimmed main piece.

**4** Pin corded piping around all the edges on the right side of the trimmed main piece, clipping the seam allowance of the piping where needed. Overlap the ends. Pull a little cord out of the piping and cut it off to eliminate bulk. Stitch around piping.

**5** Place remaining main piece over trimmed piece, with right sides facing and raw edges matching. Stitch, following the previous stitching, leaving an opening for turning. Clip seams. Turn pot holder to right side and press. Handsew opening closed.

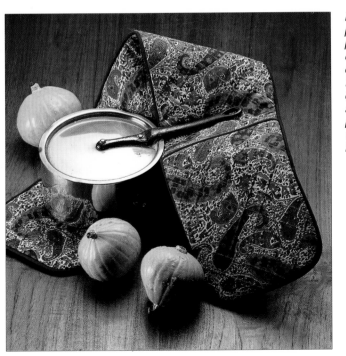

*Left: Pretty and practical, this quilted pot holder is an essential in any country kitchen. Remember to use a crisp, cotton fabric in a traditional small print and to trim it with contrasting binding*

## Tea cosy

### Before You Begin

- ❏ Measure your teapot to be sure that our tea cosy will fit. Adjust the size if necessary.

### MATERIALS

- ☐ two pieces of prequilted cotton main fabric and two pieces of lining fabric each 37 cm x 28 cm, or plain fabric and polyester wadding in the same size
- ☐ 1.80 m of corded piping
- ☐ matching sewing thread

### METHOD

1 cm seams allowed throughout.

**1** Quilt fabric if necessary following instructions on HOW TO QUILT FABRIC in the box on page 84.

**2** Using a kitchen cup as a guide, round off the two top corners of each main and lining fabric piece. Pin corded piping around the edge of the right side of one main fabric piece with raw edges matching and right sides facing. Stitch piping in place. Clip seam allowance of piping where necessary, for ease.

**3** Place remaining main fabric piece over the trimmed piece, with raw edges matching and right sides facing. Stitch, following the previous stitching.

**4** Pin piping around the bottom of the right side of the main piece, with raw edges matching and ends overlapping. Pull out a little of the cord from the piping and cut it away to eliminate bulk. Stitch piping in place. Do not turn the piece to the right side.

**5** With right sides facing and raw edges matching, stitch lining pieces together around the sides and top edge. Do not turn lining to the right side. Place lower edges of the main piece and the lining together, with right sides facing and raw edges matching. Be sure to align the side seams. Stitch around the lower edge, following the previous stitching, leaving an opening for turning. Turn the tea cosy to the right side through the opening. Handsew opening closed. Push the lining up into the main piece. Attach lining to the main fabric along the seamline with invisible hand stitches.

# Table napkin

## MATERIALS

- ☐ one 50 cm square each of main cotton fabric and of contrasting cotton fabric
- ☐ 2.10 m of corded piping
- ☐ matching sewing thread
- ☐ 50 cm of bias binding in the same colour as the corded piping for the napkin tie

## METHOD

**1** Using a kitchen cup as a guide, round off the corners of the main and contrast fabric pieces.

**2** Make the napkin in the same way as the place mat, omitting the quilting.

**3** Fold the bias binding over double lengthways, with wrong sides facing and the folded edges matching. Stitch along folded edges. Knot the ends. Stitch the centre of the bias binding 12.5 cm down from one corner.

**4** Fold the side with the tie attached in half, with wrong sides facing. Roll the opposite side of the napkin towards the end with the tie. Wrap the tie around the rolled napkin and tie into a bow.

---

# Place mat

## MATERIALS

- ☐ one piece of prequilted main fabric 50 cm x 34 cm or plain fabric and polyester wadding in the same size
- ☐ one piece of backing fabric in the main fabric or a contrasting one, 50 cm x 34 cm
- ☐ 1.80 m of corded piping
- ☐ matching sewing thread

## METHOD

**1** Quilt fabric if necessary following instructions on HOW TO QUILT FABRIC in the box on this page.

**2** Using a kitchen cup as a guide, round off the corners of the main and backing fabric pieces. With right sides facing and raw edges matching, pin piping around

*Above: Carry through your country kitchen decorating scheme into this matched set of quilted tea cosy, place mat and napkin. You can choose to use the same fabric as your curtains, as we have done, or you can complement your curtains with another small print in toning colours*

quilted main piece, clipping the seam allowance at curves for ease. Overlap the ends of the piping. Draw out a little cord from the piping and cut it off to eliminate bulk. Stitch piping in place.

**3** Place the backing piece over the main piece, with edges matching and the right sides facing. Stitch around the edge, following the previous stitching line and leaving an opening for turning the place mat. Turn the place mat to the right side through the opening. Handsew the opening closed with small, invisible stitches. Press place mat.

---

## HOW TO QUILT FABRIC

You can quilt your own fabric with your sewing machine, using a quilter's guide to plan the squares and spaces. The guide looks like an arm that extends from behind the sewing machine's presser foot into the centre of the machine.

The first row of stitching is made, then the quilter's guide is adjusted to sit along this stitching. Further rows of stitching are made, each one the same distance from the previous one, as measured by the quilter's guide.

It's an easy way to achieve professional-looking quilting and you can still use ornate machine stitches or twin-needle stitches for your quilting.

# Sideboard Drawer Divider

Are your heirlooms in a clutter? Consider dividing your sideboard drawer into made-to-measure sections to neatly contain its contents.

First measure your drawer and cutlery, then draw up a plan of how best to divide up the drawer, allowing room for candles, bottle openers, carving knives and similar dining room needs.

Measure the inside depth of your drawer, measuring from a little below the top of the drawer to allow for adequate clearance. Work out the length of each section of your dividers.

The sections are cut from plywood strips of a suitable height, then all are nailed or glued together to create a lift-in/lift-out drawer divider.

Paint or stain your divider to complement your furniture. Line the bottom of the drawer with a layer of fine wadding or felt before fitting in the divider.

## CLEVER KITCHEN IDEAS

❏ A marble worktop for rolling dough

❏ Cupboards that open to reveal a pull-out filing device for holding baking trays and muffin pans

❏ Shallow drawers for cutters, rolling pins and so on

❏ An extension table or fold-away shelf for an electric mixer, slightly lower than worktop height for easy viewing

❏ A simple stand for a recipe book

❏ A wall-mounted microwave oven on a swing-out bracket

❏ A telephone extension close by to avoid flour-coated calls

Board

Slat

screw &
glue to board

Inside
width of
drawer

# Child's Activity Top

How often do the little ones want to have fun helping out in the kitchen but the bench is too high for them?

Make this special activity top to fit over one of your kitchen drawers at kiddie height. Your child will have a workbench for painting, cutting out or assisting the master chef at those crucial moments in the kitchen.

Made quite simply from plywood, following this plan, the top can be removed and stored away when not in use.

# Wine Rack

*This project is a simple storage idea which can be adapted to the space available. The wine rack shown here will hold five dozen bottles and is built using knock-down fittings which can easily be dismantled.*

Above: Make this simple but effective wine rack in just a few hours
Left: Wire mesh being fitted to the prepared poles

## MATERIALS

- ☐ 200 mm x 25 mm pine, one of 1 x 1.50 m, two of 1.20 m
- ☐ 100 mm x 100 mm galvanised steel reinforcing mesh, two of 600 mm x 1000 mm
- ☐ 8 knockdown joint blocks
- ☐ 250 mL polyurethane
- ☐ 250 mL black self-priming epoxy paint or a black spray can

## SPECIAL TOOLS NEEDED

- ☐ bolt cutters
- ☐ 8 mm drill bit

## METHOD

**1** Cut the steel reinforcing mesh to the dimension of 6 x 10 holes using bolt cutters. The bars are approximately 5.5 mm thick. The bottom edge can be a factory edge without projections. If the bolt cutters are held against the side of the adjacent bar, you will achieve a 5 mm projection for fixing into the timber.

**2** Paint the mesh black. The job will take several hours by brush. It will be much quicker if you use a spray can, but overspray may present a problem. Make sure you protect walls with drop sheets or spray outside.

**3** Cut the sides to length, allowing for the wire mesh, the bottom shelf and ground clearance. Total length is 1100 mm. The bottom shelf should be 600 mm plus 5.5 mm, say 606 mm. The top will overhang the sides slightly, and so is cut to 665 mm.

**4** On the two sides, mark in two lines 20 mm from the front and the back. Down that line from the top, mark 3 mm, 103 mm, 203 mm, 303 mm and so on to allow for the ten bays. On the top piece, the rows of holes are set back by 5 mm, therefore 25 mm from the front and 15 mm from the rear.

**5** Oversized 8 mm holes can now be drilled to take the steel. To protect against drilling too deeply, make a drill depth stop from a scrap of 25 mm x 25 mm timber so that you only penetrate timber to 10 mm.

**6** Separate the knockdown fittings and fit the female part to the facing side of the joint, and the male part to the ends of the adjoining board. This will draw the parts together. The front blocks are fixed with the centre 50 mm from the front, and the rear ones 45 mm from the rear.

**7** Assemble the unit with the bottom shelf first; insert the mesh and then the top, being careful to align all components correctly. When finished, dismantle and clean up the timber with abrasive paper. Coat with a polyurethane or similar.

**8** When the unit is dry, you can re-assemble and stock it.

## MATERIALS

- [ ] 27 lengths of 25 mm x 25 mm DAR (PAR) softwood at 350 mm long for the legs
- [ ] 4 lengths of 25 mm x 25 mm DAR (PAR) softwood, approximately 500 mm long for the rails
- [ ] 54 mm x 32 mm x 8 gauge, counter-sunk screws
- [ ] 4 x 520 mm brass, chrome or galva-nised steel bolts, threaded full length with 2 nuts and washers to suit
- [ ] cardboard for spacers
- [ ] waterproof adhesive
- [ ] lacquer or paint

## SPECIAL TOOLS NEEDED

- [ ] tape measure
- [ ] drill
- [ ] saw
- [ ] screwdriver
- [ ] sanding block
- [ ] countersinking bit

## METHOD

**1** Cut twenty-seven legs from 25 mm x 25 mm DAR (PAR) softwood to 350 mm long.

**2** Drill a 4 mm diameter hole for the bolt 125 mm from one end of each leg. A vertical drill stand is best but it can be done carefully by hand with an electric drill.

**3** Insert the bolt into the holes and fit the nuts and washers but do not tighten them.

**4** Insert cardboard spacers (approximately 1 mm thick) between the legs and finger-tighten the bolt. (See Fig.1)

**5** Lay the assembly flat on a bench and screw and glue the top rail on at 100 mm below the top of the legs, taking care to screw only to alternate legs. (See Fig. 2)

**6** Repeat step 5 for bottom rail, attaching it 97 mm from the bottom of the legs.

**7** Turn the assembly over and repeat steps 5 and 6, this time screwing the rails to the opposite legs (i.e. legs without screws on the other side).

**8** Cut the rails to an even length where they overhang and sand them flush.

**9** Remove the cardboard spacers. Sand the plate rack and paint in your choice of colour or coat with clear lacquer.

# Plate Rack

*In any kitchen, but especially a small kitchen, where space is at a premium, it is important to make use of all available space for storage.*

*While it is simple to make, this DIY project will look smart and help keep your kitchen neat. It is suitable for novice carpenters.*

*The material is all stock size so it is readily available at your timber yard.*

*The wooden plate rack can be positioned on the sink or just next to it for handy access when washing dishes*

# New Looks for Old

Many storage-type items around the house lend themselves to renovation and will go on giving good service, so why not trade new looks for old?

When you're considering the possibilities, don't make the mistake of thinking the only way to improve the situation is to start again. Firstly, it is not always the most practical solution; secondly, the constraints of your decorating budget usually won't allow such luxury; and thirdly, in the interests of the planet, recycling should always be a priority.

Many items have exciting potential. Take that battered tin trunk in the garage, or that storage chest that has seen better days. On the following pages, you will see how they can be transformed in ways that not only add an attractive focus to your home, but also increase storage space.

In fact, once you start looking at old pieces of furniture, you will agree that they simply don't make them like that anymore! The high cost of materials and labour has led to shortcuts and, despite the greater variety available today, it has also led to the demise (in all but the most finely crafted) of the cupboard that closes perfectly and the drawer that glides shut.

## Talking timber

Timber is a rapidly diminishing resource. We should all aim to protect the world's diminishing forests by retaining and restoring old wooden pieces.

There are two ways to tackle the task of renovating timber storage pieces:
❏ Restoration – whereby the style of the piece is retained and the original finish restored.
❏ Revamping – whereby the original form of the item is retained but its finish and character is completely altered.

Workbench from Country Form

Tin from Country Form

88

The other method of cleaning up the surface is by sanding, beginning with a coarse grade of sandpaper and gradually using finer and finer grades. It is hard work but very rewarding.

## Revamping

A smooth timber surface provides you with a clean canvas for a whole range of finishes which can totally transform the piece. Painted finishes are ideal for lower quality timbers and timber veneers. The feature, *Paint Finishes* on page 32, will tell you all you need to know to get started. Don't forget that you don't need to give an all-over finish for it to be effective – explore the possibilities of stencilling and outlining as well.

## Restoration

There is a great revival of interest in old-style, antique or rustic furniture and reasonably priced pieces are becoming hard to find. All the more reason to 'rescue' one you come across, tucked away in a second-hand store (or your garage!).

Generally, the first step to restoration is the stripping of the existing surface. If you want to get right back to raw timber, you may need to use a professional stripping service. If it is quite a small piece, you can strip it using one of the many commercial products available. Always test a small, hidden area first.

*Far left: An industrial work bench makes an interesting display feature*
*Left: An old galvanised tin has been painted and stencilled to give it a new lease of life*
*Above: Second-hand shop bargains, stripped and stained like this cabinet, greatly increase their value*
*Right: A simple wooden cupboard has been stencilled and 'lined' to give it a new character*

# Clever Ways to Recycle
### FEATURE

Old or antique furniture was usually made from quality timber and had a craftsman-like finish. Furniture makers of yesteryear had time to create well-designed pieces that were both functional and very stylish. These qualities alone make furniture recycling worthwhile.

Modern lifestyles and changing needs also demand a practical and often ingenious approach to home furnishing, especially where storage is concerned. When you are on a shoestring budget and have minimal or odd spaces to play with, you need to carefully assess how and where a piece of furniture will fit in. So find yourself some wonderful, old or down-at-heel treasure and start by analysing its potential.

Does it have 'good bones'? Look beyond the shabby outward appearance of an object for fresh new refurbishing ideas – for example, the basic bookcase. It may be covered with peeling paint, look uninteresting and, as it stands, certainly wouldn't fit in with a fresh, bright furnishing look. However, once it has been repaired, stripped and perhaps stained or repainted, there are many decorative and practical ways of using it.

You could fix it to a wall above floor level and make a set of feature shelves; use it as a bedhead or a room divider; fit it into or in front of a no-longer-used doorway to display a treasured collection; place it in the garage for extra tool storage; cut it into two lower units and seal it with paint to make an accessible pot-plant stand; or stand it in a hanging-only cupboard as storage for folded clothes and shoes. Your once-shabby bookcase can be transformed in even more subtle ways by covering it completely with wallpaper or fabric to blend in with the rest of your decor. The list goes on – and this was only a humble bookcase!

Once you enter into the spirit of searching for unwanted treasures, you will begin to see possibilities in just about any piece of furniture. But beware, it's important to recognise the strengths and weaknesses of your 'find'.

Thinking about buying and refurbishing an old cupboard? There are many real advantages in doing-up an old cupboard: good-quality timber and workmanship, spacious deep drawers and generous hanging capacity, for example. There are, alas, some potential drawbacks:

❏ Is the timber used heavily lacquered? This may be a real problem to strip and restain; in this case you may be forced to paint over the lacquer.

❏ Is it solid and free of insect attack? Look for tell-tale small holes and piles of sawdust. Professional fumigation may be required, or treatment with woodworm fluid and polish to restore the surface.

❏ Does it have door hinges and locks? These can be replaced but often not cheaply. Quality brass fittings can be expensive at retail outlets, so shop around. Brass

*Left and below: A set of stacked cane suitcases are a great recycling idea. Paint them inside and out with gloss spray paint in a bright colour.*
*To dress up your suitcases, simply line the inside of the lid and the suitcase with polyester wadding, gluing the edges to secure. Cover the wadding with a pretty print fabric, gluing it in place.*

*A rummage in the garden shed revealed this well-shaped old tin trunk. It was not rusty and only needed to have the old paint removed to prepare it for its new life. It was painted with undercoat and paint suitable for metal and the design was added using a commercial stencil and spray paints. Take care to screen the area with cardboard to prevent excess paint escaping and drifting where it is not needed.*

restoration experts often have oddments available, and are well worth visiting.

❏ Do the drawers run smoothly? You may need to replace the drawer runners or use sandpaper to smooth off damp-swollen timber.

❏ Can you get the cupboard through the door when moving it to its new address? If the tape measure says this is not to be, is it possible to unscrew parts of the cupboard and reassemble it once moved?

Visit auctions, fairs, church bazaars and garage sales. Check the newspaper often for auctions of office furniture (you'll be surprised by the variety and the bargains!). Two second-hand identical filing cabinets, perhaps repainted then set apart by about 1.50 m with a wide softwood table top resting across the tops, makes a fine desk. If no old table top is available, consider buying a new one from contemporary knockdown furniture suppliers.

Remember that opportunities often present themselves in obscure and unpredictable ways. To help you with your treasure hunt, consider how different pieces of furniture can be adapted:

❏ Tables can have legs shortened to become casual occasional tables. They are perfect for stencilling or covering with fabric, and are a natural for a simple paint-over.

❏ Strongly woven baskets provide all sorts of storage possibilities: paint them, line them with fabric, stack lidded baskets, or use them in rows on open shelves for kitchen storage. Flat baskets with rims can become excellent trays. Old cane laundry baskets make ideal toy storage and can easily become a decorative feature when cleverly coloured. A deep, strongly woven basket with handles can be both stylish and practical when filled with wood ready for an open fire. Leave it outside under shelter for wood storage all year round, and carry it in when the weather sends smoke signals.

❏ Old luggage can provide decorative storage. Paint tin trunks, restain old leather luggage or refurbish a truly authentic hatbox.

❏ Boxes of all sorts and sizes can become amusing and talked-about storage containers (or articles). Old wooden ammunition boxes, biscuit tins, sturdy paper cartons and slatted pine fruit boxes can be painted or decoupaged, and even shoe boxes made from very firm cardboard can be covered with fabric to become practical and attractive storage containers.

❏ Picture frames can be used as noticeboard surrounds.

❏ Small wooden safety ladders, providing they have a flat top, can become ideal bedside tables. Single-sided old ladders with frame and rungs of dowel can become discussion pieces when used as towel racks in a kitchen – lean them against a wall and you instantly have storage for as many towels as you could need.

❏ Storage is an essential element in any household, but don't be bogged down by the expected or expensive solutions. The whimsical, achievable, recycled, amusing and unexpected alternatives are just waiting to be discovered.

# Bathroom
## beauties

With a frill here, a stencil there and a few metres of pretty fabric, you can give your existing bathroom a bright new look – and it won't break the bank.

Begin with a drawn plan and some idea of a new colour scheme – though you may have to accept the limitations of the existing colours of the tiles and other fittings. The soft pink and white colour scheme of this bathroom is carried through in the shower curtain, festoon blind, basin skirting and wall stencilling. Avoid the introduction of too many colours, so as not to add clutter to a less-than-generously proportioned bathroom. Remember, the fabric and trimmings you choose will have to withstand the damp environment of the bathroom. Check with your supplier before you buy to avoid disappointment later.

# Festoon Blind

*For a soft, romantic look, nothing beats festoon blinds. The fabric you choose will set the style for your blind, from the soft and feminine look of sheer lace to the charm of this crisp cotton.*

## Before You Begin

❏ To calculate how much fabric you need, measure the width and length of the window and multiply each measurement by two. If you need to join two pieces of fabric to achieve the right width, do so with small, flat seams.

❏ If you are going to trim your blind with a frill, you will need twice the distance to be covered by the frill, a length of purchased piping (or make your own) equal to that distance and bias binding as long as the frill.

MATERIALS

☐ sufficient fabric for the blind and the frill (see *Before You Begin*)
☐ sufficient matching bias binding
☐ sufficient matching piping
☐ length of pencil pleating tape, which draws up to the width of your window
☐ ring tape, four times the length of your blind
☐ curtain track, the width of your window
☐ curtain rod, the width of your window
☐ brackets for the rod

METHOD

See the Pull Out Pattern Sheet at the back of the book for the cord threading diagram.

1 Cut a strip of fabric 18 cm x the length required for your blind, for the frill.

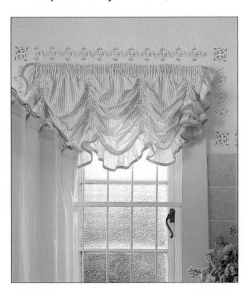

Bind one long edge of the strip with bias binding. Gather the other edge to the length required to fit around the sides and lower edge of the blind.

2 Baste the piping around the side and lower edges of the right side of the fabric piece (or joined pieces) with raw edges matching. Pin the frill to the edge, over the top of the piping, with raw edges matching and right sides facing. Stitch through all thicknesses. Press the seam allowances towards the blind. Stitch again in the gutter of the piping, securing the seam allowance.

3 Turn in 2.5 cm on the top edge of the blind and the frill. Press. Unravel the draw cords of the first 5 cm of the pencil pleating tape. Pin the upper edge of the tape to the top of your blind, 1.5 cm from the edge. Stitch down all edges of the tape, stitching the top hem as you go. Do not draw up the cords.

4 Stitch the ring tape down the sides of the blind, just inside the frill, and at two equally spaced points across the blind from top to bottom hems. Leave an extra 6 cm of tape at the bottom of each length. See the cord-threading diagram for the location of the cords.

5 Loop this tape back on itself so that the end is just above the hem. Stitch. These loops are to hold the bottom rod.

6 Gather the pencil pleating cord, until the blind gathers to the width of the curtain track.

7 Attach the eyelets to the window frame, just below the track, to correspond with the top of each strip of ring tape, and another, just below one curtain track bracket, through which you will thread the blind cords.

8 Cut a cord for each strip of ring tape, long enough to reach from the bottom rod, up the blind, through the eyelets, across the top and down to the side where the extra eyelet is, leaving sufficient length for knotting them together below the eyelet.

9 Loop the rings together as you go to form a permanent blousing effect. Attach the blind to the curtain track with the hooks. Insert the rod through the tape loops at the lower edge of the blind.

# Basin Skirting

*These simple-to-make panels of fabric can hide unsightly plumbing and even create new storage space, as the space they conceal can contain shelving. As there are countless shapes and sizes for bathroom basins/units there is no precise pattern for making it – rather we give a method for making the frill, with several variations for fixing it in place.*

## Before You Begin

❏ First measure the depth and width of the frill. If you plan to gather the fabric, allow double the width needed. If you take advantage of a pattern in the fabric, such as these stripes, to form pleats, work out the width of pleated fabric required. The striped panel holds the pleats in place.

❏ Don't forget to make a split in a suitable place for access to the storage space behind. You can achieve this by making your frill in two sections so that each can be drawn back as needed.

❏ Consider using the same fabric to make shower curtains and frilled blinds. A truly coordinated look can work wonders in an otherwise basic bathroom!

MATERIALS

☐ sufficient fabric
☐ elastic
☐ cup hooks
☐ small rings

METHOD

1 Establish how you are going to secure the frill, as this will have a bearing on the style. Rounded basins on a pedestal can have a frill with a casing, allowing strong elastic to be threaded through it. The ends of the elastic are hooked over two cup hooks fixed to the wall on either

side of the basin at the height of the casing. The frill will naturally gather onto the elastic.

2 Pleats work well with basin units, where there are angles like this one. Screw cup hooks into the wall at the height of the striped panel, and again in the concave angle. Add more hooks elsewhere if it seems appropriate. Pleat the fabric to fit exactly. Attach small rings by hand at the back of the stitched panel to coincide with the hooks.

# Shower Cap

## MATERIALS
- [ ] 60 cm of 115 cm wide cotton fabric
- [ ] 60 cm of 115 cm wide plastic sheeting
- [ ] 2 lengths of bias binding, each 2 m long (one could be self fabric)
- [ ] 1 cm wide elastic

## METHOD

1 Cut two circles 60 cm in diameter, one from the cotton fabric and one from the plastic sheeting.

2 Place the plastic circle against the wrong side of the cotton fabric. Stitch around the outside edge. Trim both fabric and plastic close to the stitching.

3 Bind the joined edges of the circles with self-fabric bias binding, turning in the raw ends where they meet.

4 Stitch the second length of bias binding 6 cm from the edge, on the plastic side, to form the casing for the elastic.

5 Thread the elastic through the casing. Check the fit before joining the ends of the elastic.

# Toilet Roll Holder

## MATERIALS
- [ ] two strips of cotton fabric, each 90 cm x 14 cm
- [ ] iron-on interfacing, 90 cm x 14 cm
- [ ] strip of fabric, 12 cm x 3 cm for the loop
- [ ] 3.20 m of 1.5 cm wide lace edging
- [ ] 1.30 m of 3 mm wide satin ribbon
- [ ] small wooden curtain ring
- [ ] craft glue

## METHOD

1 Iron the interfacing onto the wrong side of one fabric strip. Trim both strips of fabric to a point at one end.

2 Stitch two rows of lace down the centre of the interfaced strip so that the straight edges of the lace meet in the middle. Stitch a length of ribbon over the line where the laces join.

3 With right sides together and raw edges matching, stitch lace all around the lace-trimmed piece, pleating the lace at the point and the corners for ease.

4 Place both fabric pieces together with right sides facing and raw edges matching. Stitch, following the previous stitching line and leaving the straight end open. Trim the fabric at the points and corners. Turn to the right side and press.

5 Turn under 1 cm at the open end, fold this end to the back and slipstitch to the back of the holder with the corners matching.

6 Fold the strip for the loop over lengthways with right sides together. Stitch along the long side. Turn and press. Topstitch along the length with four rows of stitching.

7 Wind the ribbon around the curtain ring to cover it, gluing the ends to secure them. Fold the strip for the loop

*Toiletry bag, toilet roll holder and shower cap*

Left: The bathroom showing the shower curtain, festoon bind and trimmed towels
Below: Detail of the wooden bathmat showing the cord threaded through plastic tubing

# Shower Curtain

*This shower curtain is totally decorative, covering a purely functional, plastic shower curtain already in place.*

## MATERIALS

☐ sufficient fabric to cover the existing curtain. Plastic curtains are not hemmed at sides and lower edge, so be sure to allow extra fabric for 5 cm deep side and lower hems, and the 10 cm turnover at the top. If necessary, join fabric lengths together with flat seams to achieve the desired size.
☐ matching sewing thread

## METHOD

1 Fold in 1 cm on the sides, then fold another 4 cm. Press and stitch. Fold up the lower hem and stitch in the same way. Fold over 5 cm at the top then fold another 5 cm. Stitch along the first fold.

2 Make buttonholes for the curtain rings at the same intervals as they are on the plastic shower curtain. Hang the fabric curtain on the outside of the plastic one by pushing the hooks through the button-holes of both curtains at once.

3 If you wish to hook the fabric curtain out of the way or tie it to one side, you can purchase a suitable water-resistant cord and tassel and attach a hook to the wall at the appropriate height.

# Trimmed Towels

*Across the ends of most towels is a flat, woven band. This is the ideal place to stitch rows of ribbon or braid. You can also stitch lace or scalloped trims under the edge of a length of ribbon or fabric.*

*Remember to trim your face cloths, bathmats and hand towels for a truly coordinated look in your bathroom.*

around the ring over the ribbon ends. Glue the ends of the loop. Slipstitch the loop to the point on the wrong side of the holder. Tie a small bow and attach it as shown.

8 Stitch across the holder, halfway between the handsewing and the lower folded edge, dividing it into two compartments.

# Toiletry Bag

## MATERIALS

☐ 60 cm x 28 cm cotton fabric
☐ 60 cm x 28 cm plastic sheeting
☐ 1.60 m of 12 mm wide satin ribbon

## METHOD

1 Fold the fabric over lengthways with right sides together. Stitch the sides. Do the same with the plastic.

2 Turn the fabric bag right side out. Trim 5 cm from the top edge of the plastic bag. Slip the plastic bag inside the fabric bag.

3 Turn in 6 mm at the top edge of the fabric bag. Turn under another 5 cm to cover the top edge of the plastic bag. Stitch through all thicknesses at the fold and again 1.5 cm away to form the casing.

4 Open the stitching of the side seams between the casing lines. Cut the length of ribbon in half. Thread one half in one opening, through the casing and out the same opening. Repeat with the other half of the ribbon at the other opening. Knot the ribbon ends together.

# Bath Mat

*This is a terrific solution to the perennial problem of soggy bath mats. An occasional scrub-down and an airing are all that are needed.*

## Before You Begin

❏ Decide what size bath mat you can accommodate in your bathroom before purchasing materials. Our mat measures 45 cm x 58 cm. Remember when you are measuring, that the plastic tubing makes a 2 cm gap between each piece of timber.

### MATERIALS

☐ 10 lengths of dressed (planed) pine, each 4 cm wide x 2 cm thick x 45 cm long
☐ 1 m of non-perishing plastic tubing, 14 mm in diameter
☐ 2 m of 12 mm diameter nylon rope
☐ electric drill with 16 mm and 13 mm diameter drill bits
☐ pencil or chalk for marking

### METHOD

**1** Cut timber to size if necessary. Line up the lengths side by side on their 2 cm sides and rule a line 10 cm in from each end across all the timber sides. Turn the timber lengths over and repeat on the other side for accurate drill positions. Mark the halfway point in the length of each piece of timber on this line.

**2** Drill right through each timber piece at centre marking, using the small bit. Then drill through the same hole with the larger bit, drilling only to a depth of 1.5 cm. Repeat on the other side.

**3** Cut the plastic tubing into 5 cm lengths. These will be used to separate the timber pieces. Starting at one end, thread the rope through one piece of timber and then one length of plastic tubing, then the next piece of timber and another piece of plastic tubing. Work along one row of holes, out the opposite end and back through the remaining row of holes on the other side. Knot the ends of the rope securely. Hold the knots over a lighted match to fuse the ends and stop them from fraying.

# New Life for Old Tiles

If your bathroom works perfectly well but you can't stand the colour of the tiles – you have a problem. Re-tiling is costly, so some camouflage is necessary. You may, of course, choose wallpaper that is complementary – so that the choice of tiles looks quite deliberate. If wallpaper does not appeal, read on for three other clever solutions to the problem.

## Painting tiles

It is possible to paint tiles, as you would a wall, if you prepare the surface carefully. First, wash down the tiles with sugar soap or white spirit to totally remove all traces of soap scum. When the tiles are clean and dry, apply a sealer coat of a paint-on waterproofing material, such as a Bond Crete or Uni-Bond. This provides a surface to which paint will cling. Paint over the sealer coat with your chosen colour of vinyl gloss, painting over the grouting as well. You can even add a stencilled or painted border around the top of the tiles.

## Etching a pattern

Make or purchase a stencil of your choice. You could use one from the Pull Out Pattern Sheet at the back of this book. Position the stencil and draw around the outlines using a chinagraph pencil (it will draw on shiny surfaces). Using a small paintbrush, fill in the outlines of the design with acid etching paste, available from hardware, stained glass or sheet glass suppliers. Allow it to dry for at least two hours. Then wash off the dried paste with water. What remains is a shadowy outline of the design. This is a very subtle effect.

## Etching and painting a pattern

Once you have designed a pattern as instructed in *Etching a pattern*, you can paint over the etched area with cold ceramic paints take many hours to dry – or cure – and it will be at least two or three weeks before they are thoroughly cured. They are touch-dry in an hour or so, but take care to avoid scratching the design until it is fully cured. You can use the bathroom in the meantime, but the drying process may be prolonged by the resulting dampness. If you do not etch first, draw on the design using a chinagraph pencil and fill in with cold ceramic paints. Regardless of whether you etch first, seal the entire painted area with ceramic sealer, (available from hardware stores) after the paint is dry.

# Bedtime
## stories

*I*n days past, bedrooms were often
the forgotten rooms in the house,
at least as far as decorating was
concerned – but no more! These days
the decor of most bedrooms revolves
around the wonderful array of bed
linens available. You can dress up the
most uninspiring room with clever use
of fabric for sheets, pillowcases and
quilt. And don't forget to carry the
theme through into curtains or blinds
to match.

Making your own bed linen is easy,
lets you create your own decorating
scheme and can save you money too!
Remember to measure the bed carefully
– small differences won't matter for
flat sheets, but accuracy is important
for ruffles or valances.

Laura Ashley (Australia) Pty Limited

# Down to DETAIL

## Stencilled Bedhead, Cushions and Quilt

*You don't need to be rich or an artist to own this original work of art! Add a little ingenuity and some stylish paintwork and you can make this bedhead yourself! The bedhead is actually an old picture frame, surrounding a stencilled fabric panel which matches the stencilled quilt. These long narrow frames were commonly available during the 1920s and are usually solidly constructed of lightly carved wood. You could make a similar frame for yourself. The moulded timber pieces are usually available at specialist timber shops, or perhaps a professional picture framer could advise you.*

*As to which design you stencil, that's entirely up to you. There are a number of designs on the Pull Out Pattern Sheet at the back of this book or a variety of prepared stencils can be purchased or make your own from any design or pattern that pleases you.*

## Bedhead

### MATERIALS

- ☐ one large rectangular, wooden frame in good condition
- ☐ sufficient cotton fabric to fit into the frame, allowing approximately 10 cm around all the edges for fastening to the frame
- ☐ manila card for the stencil
- ☐ turps (white spirit)
- ☐ linseed oil
- ☐ coloured pencils
- ☐ sharp craft knife
- ☐ board for cutting stencil on
- ☐ stencilling paints and brushes
- ☐ a staple gun or strong sewing needle and thread
- ☐ piece of firm backing board and thick polyester wadding, each the size of the inside measurement of the frame
- ☐ 3 cm wide masking tape
- ☐ wide, thick brown paper
- ☐ 2 eye hooks and wire for hanging the frame
- ☐ small tacks and a hammer

### METHOD

See Page 103 for the large stencil and the Pull Out Pattern Sheet at the back of the book for the small one.

**For the stencilled fabric:**
Following directions on page 101, stencil the design onto the fabric so that the motifs sit evenly within the frame. Allow it to dry thoroughly. Press on the wrong side.

**For making the frame:**

1 Press in and sew a 1 cm hem all around fabric.

2 Place the wadding over the backing board. You may need to tape it into place temporarily. Place the stencilled fabric over wadding, positioning it so that the design is in its right position. Tape the fabric edges to the wrong side of the board, checking that you have not distorted the fabric. Staple the fabric edges to the backing board, or stitch the edges together from top to bottom and then from side to side, using a handsewing needle and strong thread. Pull the thread firmly to keep the fabric in place.

**3** Place the covered board into the frame, hammering in small tacks on the back around the frame's inner edge to keep the covered board in place.

**4** Cover the back of the board with brown paper, folded or cut to size. Cover the edges of the paper with masking tape, taking the tape onto the back of the frame as well. Insert the eye hooks into each side of the frame at the back. Check the required length for the hanging wire. Wind the ends of the wire securely around the eye hooks. Hang the frame at a suitable height above the bed.

# Quilt cover

| Before You Begin |
| --- |

❑ This quilt cover is designed for a single bed. The same method can be used to make a larger cover simply by increasing the number of stencilled panels used.

## MATERIALS

**For the quilt cover:**
☐ 7.5 m of 90 cm wide calico or 4 m of 137 cm wide calico
☐ 5.5 m of 112 cm wide homespun cotton in a contrasting colour to match or complement your chosen stencil colour
☐ 60 cm of continuous zipper or two 30 cm dress zippers
☐ manila card for making the stencil
☐ craft knife or sharp, pointed blade
☐ stencil brushes or sponges, one for each colour
☐ cutting board for cutting stencil on
☐ linseed oil
☐ mineral turpentine (white spirit)
☐ stencilling paints

## METHOD
See Pull Out Pattern Sheet at the back of the book for the floral stencil design.

**For the stencilling:**
**1** Coat the manila card with a 50:50 mixture of mineral turpentine (white spirit) and linseed oil. Allow it to dry.

**2** Trace the design onto the card and cut it out with the sharp knife. You can cut both leaf and flower designs on the one card.

**3** Cut the main fabric into twelve squares each 49 cm x 49 cm. Fold each square

## Stencilled cushion

### MATERIALS
- [ ] one 40 cm square of main fabric to be stencilled for the front, two pieces 22 cm x 40 cm for cushion back
- [ ] 30 cm zipper
- [ ] contrast fabric strip 1.60 m x 8 cm for border
- [ ] contrast fabric strip 3.20 m x 22 cm for ruffle
- [ ] 40 cm cushion insert

### METHOD
1 cm seams allowed throughout.

**1** Stencil the same floral motif as the quilt onto the cushion front, following the stencilling instructions on page 101.

**2** Cut the 8 cm wide contrast strip into four 40 cm lengths, then cut each end of each strip at a perfect diagonal. Join the four strips into an open square by seaming the corners together, stopping the stitching on each corner 1 cm from the inner edge. Turn in 1 cm on the inner edges of the square, press.

**3** Place the border square onto the stencilled front, with the wrong side of the square facing the right side of the cushion front and matching raw edges. Baste along inner edges of the border square, then stitch through all thicknesses.

**4** Join short ends of 22 cm wide strip to form a circle. Fold the strip in half lengthways, with wrong sides together. Divide the strip into quarters and mark with pins, having the seam as one quarter point. Gather along the raw edges. Draw up the gathering. Pin the ruffle to the right side of the front, with a quarter point at each corner, right sides facing and raw edges matching. Stitch through all thicknesses just inside the gathering.

**5** Join back pieces along 40 cm edge, using a 2 cm seam allowance and leaving a 30 cm opening for the zipper in the middle. Press seams open. Insert the zipper into the opening. Open the zipper.

**6** Pin the back to the front with right sides facing, keeping the ruffle out of the way. Stitch around the edge. Trim the corners. Turn the cushion cover right side out through the zipper opening. Place cushion insert inside cover.

---

in half, then in half again. Mark the fold point – this is the centre of your square.

**4** Place a fabric square on a flat surface, suitable for painting on. Hold it in place with pins or tape. Position your stencil on the fabric square. Paint one colour version of the design onto six squares and the other six squares with the second colour. Allow them to dry, then iron on the wrong side with a medium to hot, dry iron, to set the paint.

**For the sewing:**
1 cm seams allowed throughout and all pieces of the quilt are joined with right sides facing and raw edges even.

**Note:** Fabric strips A, B and C have been specified approximately 10 cm longer to allow for fabric movement during sewing. You may prefer to add a little more. The back of the quilt is cut out once the front is finished and can be measured accurately.

**1** Cut the contrasting homespun fabric into the following strips: two pieces each 7 cm x 2.15 m for A, two pieces each 7 cm x 1.60 m for B, two pieces each 7 cm x 2.10 m for C, 9 pieces 7 cm x 49 cm for D.

**2** Lay out the printed squares in three rows of four in alternating colours. Position the squares so that the stems of one colour hang 'down' the quilt and the stems of the other colour point 'up' the quilt. Starting with the first vertical row of four squares, and using three of the D strips, join the squares into a long panel,

with a D strip separating each one. Keep the layout of the squares in mind when joining the strips to the squares. Press all seams towards the strips. Repeat this procedure with the other two rows of four squares, again checking that your squares have remained according to your layout.

**3** Connect the first complete long panel to the second one with one of the C strips, and then the second to the third with the other C strip.

**4** Sew the B strips along the top and bottom of the quilt, then sew the A strips along both sides.

**5** If necessary, recut the edges of your quilt front to make them straight. Measure the quilt front, and cut the backing piece to the same width as the front but 3 cm longer.

**6** Cut across the backing strip 12 cm up from the lower edge. Rejoin these pieces in a 1.5 cm seam, leaving a 60 cm opening in the middle for the zipper or zippers. Press the seam open. Insert the zipper. If you are using two dress zippers, sew them so that the pull tabs are in the centre of the opening. When they are both pulled back, the opening will be of sufficient size to insert the quilt.

**7** Place the back and front together, with right sides facing and stitch around the edges. Turn the quilt cover to the right side through the zipper opening.

*This is the larger stencil outline for the pillows, bedhead and the floorcloth. See the Pull Out*
*Pattern at the back of the book for the quilt stencil and the smaller floral stencil*

# Bed Linen

❏ Sheeting fabrics are most appropriate for making bed linen. Cotton dress fabrics are also ideal but you will have to sew lengths together to achieve the correct size. Use flat seams for this purpose, being sure to conceal raw edges. Sheeting fabric widths vary from 228 cm to 250 cm, from selvage to selvage. The quantities given in our charts (see Pull Out Pattern Sheet at the back of the book) relate to these widths, calculated on standard sizes of manufactured sheets and quilt covers.

❏ All our sheets and quilt covers are cut with selvages at the top and bottom while the side edges have been hemmed. However check your own bed measurements before you begin. You may have to reverse this arrangement and have the selvages on the sides and hems at the top and bottom. Dress fabrics should be joined with seams running vertically down the sheet or quilt cover so selvages will be on the sides and top and bottom are hemmed.

❏ Make your quilt cover to fit your quilt, allowing some ease. Measure your own quilt before purchasing materials. Consider using contrasting fabrics for the front and back of your quilt, making it reversible.

## Quilt cover

### MATERIALS

❏ sufficient fabric for your quilt, allowing for front and back
❏ some form of closure, such as a zipper or a hook and loop tape, such as Velcro. If no zipper is available that is long enough, sew in two long dress zippers, with their pulltags at the centre. When both zippers are open, the space is large enough to insert quilt
❏ matching sewing thread

### METHOD

1 cm seams allowed throughout.

**1** If using sheeting, place the selvages at the top and bottom edges. If using cotton craft fabrics, join lengths with flat seams, to achieve the overall size required for the front and back.

**2** Place front and back pieces together with right sides facing. If you are using a zipper to close the quilt cover, join front to back at both ends of one short side using a 1.5 cm seam, leaving the correct opening for your zipper. Press seam allowance open. Insert zipper and open it.

**3** Place front and back together so that right sides are facing. Sew right around the edges, using a 1 cm seam.

**4** Turn the quilt cover to the right side through the open zipper.

## Bed ruffle or valance

❏ It is difficult to give exact measurements and fabric quantities for a bed ruffle as beds are of so many different heights. The base or flat part of the ruffle is the same size as the mattress top plus seam allowances. The frill is the same depth as the height of bed base from floor, plus hem and seam allowances. It should be 4 times as long as the bed length plus 4 times the bed width.

### METHOD

1 cm seams allowed throughout.

**1** For beds with no bed posts or footboard, simply hem bedhead end of the base fabric piece.

**2** Join frill pieces to make one continuous strip. Hem both short ends and one long edge of the frill. Gather the raw edge. Pin the gathered edge to the raw edges of the base piece with right sides together and raw edges even. Adjust gathering to fit. Stitch frill in place. Press.

**3** For beds with posts, hem the head end as above. The frill will need to be made in three sections, to begin and end on either side of the posts. Each section of the frill should be twice as long as the equivalent part of the base piece. Hem the short ends. Hem one long side of each frill piece. Gather the raw edge of each piece and pin to the edges of the base piece with right sides facing and the raw edges matching. Adjust gathers to fit. Stitch.

**4** To sew ties to fasten around the bed posts, sew 10 cm of elastic to one end

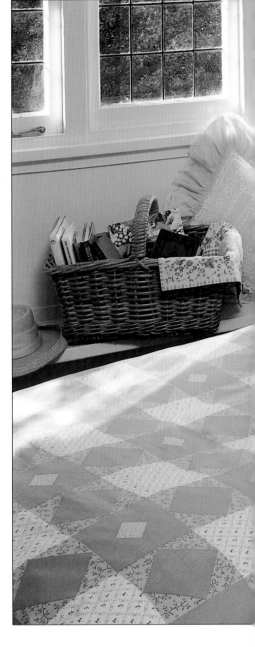

of each tie and the other end to the valance corner. This will take the strain off the ties and prevent the stitching from snapping.

## Plain pillowcase with contrast panel

### MATERIALS

❏ fabric piece 50 cm x 1.60 m
❏ contrast panel of fabric 50 cm x 15 cm
❏ 50 cm of contrast purchased bias binding or a 3 cm x 50 cm fabric strip

### METHOD

1 cm seams allowed throughout.

# Ruffled pillowcase

## MATERIALS

☐ Cut one front pillowcase piece 78 cm x 50 cm and two pillowcase back pieces, one 70 cm x 50 cm and another 22 cm x 50 cm

☐ Cut two 5.20 m long strips (join lengths if necessary) for ruffles, one 10 cm wide from the main fabric, another 12 cm wide from contrast fabric

## METHOD

1 cm seams allowed throughout.

**1** Place two ruffle strips together with right sides facing and one long edge matching. Stitch along matched long edge. Press seam flat. Fold the strip over with wrong sides facing, matching remaining long raw edges. You now have a strip with a border of contrast at the folded edge.

**2** Join the short ends of the strip to form a continuous circle. Gather the raw edges. Pin the ruffle around the edge of the pillowcase front piece, with right sides facing and raw edges matching. Stitch just outside the line of gathering.

**3** Narrow hem one 50 cm edge of each back piece. Place both back pieces on top of the front piece, with right sides facing, overlapping the hemmed edges at the centre, and with outside edges matching. Pin and baste around the outside edge.

**4** Stitch around the outside edge through all thicknesses, taking care that the frill lies flat towards the middle of the pillowcase. Turn the pillowcase to the right side and press.

**1** Turn in 1 cm on the raw edge at one 50 cm end of the main fabric piece, then turn another 1 cm. Press. Stitch. Place the contrast fabric panel at the remaining 50 cm end, with the right side of the panel facing the wrong side of the pillowcase and raw edges matching. Stitch across 50 cm end. Turn panel to the right side of the pillowcase. Press under 1 cm on the remaining raw edge of the 50 cm edge of the contrast panel.

**2** Fold bias strip over double with wrong sides together, press. Slide raw edge under pressed edge of contrast panel. Stitch through all thicknesses, securing contrast panel and bias strip to the pillowcase.

**3** Fold pillowcase as shown in the diagram on this page, with right sides

facing. Stitch sides. Take care to secure the stitching well at the open end of the pillowcase. Turn to the right side and press.

*Top: Coordinated bed linen in a patchwork of fresh colours and patterns*
*Above left: Corner of the ruffled pillowcase showing the contrast binding*
*Above right: The folding diagram for the pillowcase*

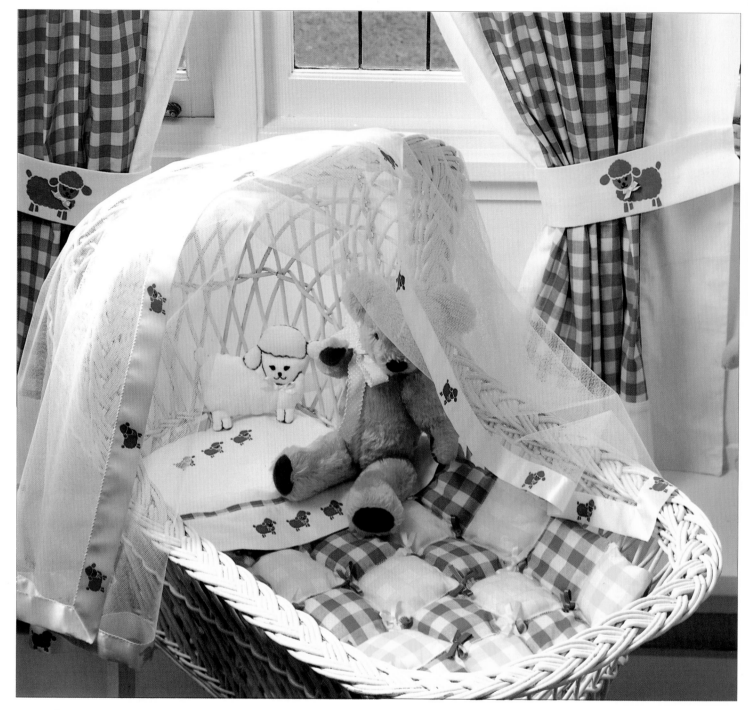

# Baby's Room

*Decorating a room for a new baby is a true labour of love. Ideally your decor should 'grow' with the baby and still be fresh in a couple of years time. This means avoiding tiny baby motifs in fabric and looking for something a little more timeless. To make the cuddly lamb toy, use the large outline on the Pull Out Pattern Sheet, enlarged to twice the size and cut two shapes from brushed fabric. Stitch around the edge with right sides facing, leaving an opening for stuffing with polyester wadding. Using embroidery stitches outline the features as indicated .The large, square net is edged with purchased satin blanket binding that has been stencilled to match the sheets.*

*Baby's room in a cheerful combination of sunny yellow and crisp blue, showing the tie backs, curtains, bassinet quilt, sheets, toy and trimmed net.*

## Trimmed curtains

| **Before You Begin** |
| --- |

❑ See the Pull Out Pattern Sheet at the back of the book for how to measure your window and estimate fabric quantities. Quantities for trimmings will depend on the size of your curtains.

❏ Decide whether you wish to have two curtains that open in the middle and are pulled to each side, or a single curtain. If two curtains are your choice, halve the width prescribed and add an extra 5 cm to each curtain for the centre hem allowances. Sewing instructions are given for one curtain, simply make two using the same method.

## MATERIALS

☐ sufficient main curtain fabric (see diagram for measuring on the Pull Out Pattern Sheet at the back of the book)
☐ three strips of contrast fabric 15 cm wide x the length of your curtains for the side panels; another piece of contrast fabric 15 cm wide x width of your main curtain plus side borders for the lower panel
☐ two strips of contrast fabric, each 15 cm x 55 cm for tie backs, one for stencilling, one for lining
☐ a piece of fusible interfacing 15 cm x 55 cm
☐ 20 cm bias binding or 3 cm wide fabric strips
☐ 2 cm diameter dowelling or a curtain pole to suit your window
☐ two support brackets and screws
☐ curtain tie back hook
☐ manila card for the stencil
☐ linseed oil
☐ mineral turpentine (white spirit)
☐ pencil
☐ sharp craft knife
☐ stencil brushes and paints
☐ cutting board

## METHOD

See Pull Out Pattern Sheet at the back of the book for the lamb stencil design. 1 cm seams allowed throughout.

**1** Place the two side panel pieces together with right sides facing. With a pencil, mark a perfect diagonal at one end. Cut off fabric along this line on both panels. Also mark and cut off perfect diagonals at both ends of the bottom contrast panel. Sew the contrast panels together at the diagonal seams, with right sides together and stopping the stitching 1 cm from the inner edge, to form a U shape. Press in 1 cm all around inner edge.

**2** Place the contrast panels on the curtain so that the right side of the contrast panels faces the wrong side of the curtain and raw edges are matching. Pin and baste. Stitch around the outside edge.

**3** Press the seam and the contrast panel to the right side of the curtain. Stitch the pressed inner edge to the curtain through all thicknesses. Press. Stencil the border now if desired.

**4** Turn in 1 cm at the top, then turn another 7 cm. Press. Stitch. Stitch again 3.5 cm from the top. This row of stitching forms the pocket for inserting a rod and will have a frilled effect when the curtain is in position.

**5** Install the brackets. Slide the curtain onto the pole, adjusting the gathers to fit. Hang the curtain.

*Stencil the curtain tie back with a lamb to match the sheets. Its features can be stencilled or embroidered and you can sew on a tiny bow as we have done*

**For the tie back:**

**1** Stencil the tie back piece following the instructions on page 101. Interface the stencilled tie back. Open out the bias binding and press flat. Fold the fabric strip or bias over double, with right sides facing and raw edges matching. Stitch the long side. Turn and press. Cut into two 10 cm pieces. Pin both ends of one length to one end of the stencilled tie back, with right sides facing and raw edges matching. Repeat for the other end with the remaining length. Place the tie back lining over the stencilled tie back. Stitch around the edges leaving an opening for turning. Turn. Press neatly.

**2** Install the hook at the appropriate height. Place the tie back around the curtain and secure by hooking the loops over the hook.

# Bassinet quilt

*This pretty cover is one of the simplest ways of constructing a quilt that we know of! With the same technique you can make quilts of any size.*

## Before You Begin

❏ You will need to work out how many squares and what size squares you will need to make up a quilt to fit your bassinet. The cover shown is 5 squares wide x 6 squares long, where each square is 12 cm x 12 cm. Each 'pillow' of the quilt has a front and a back so for a quilt like this one you will need about 50 cm each of two main fabrics that are 115 cm wide.

❏ As the quilt will need to be washable, pre-shrink all fabric before sewing.

## MATERIALS

☐ sufficient cotton or polycotton fabric
☐ polyester fibre for stuffing
☐ self-fabric rouleaux or contrasting ribbon

## METHOD

1 cm seams allowed throughout.

**1** Cut out the required number of squares from each fabric. Pair up one square from each fabric with right sides facing. Stitch around three sides leaving the remaining side open for inserting the stuffing. Clip the corners and turn the pillow right side out, making sure to push the corners out carefully. Press, turning under 1 cm on open edges.

*A close up of the bassinet quilt showing how the 'pillows' are joined*

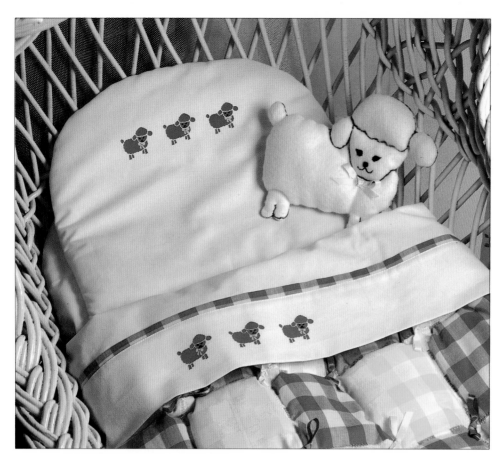

*Baby's bassinet with stencilled pillow shape, stencilled and trimmed sheet and pillow quilt. Make the fluffy lamb toy for baby to cuddle*

**2** Place the pillows in rows as determined by your quilt size, butting the edges together accurately. Sew butted edges of adjoining pillows together, using a zigzag or similar stitch.

**3** Stuff pillows, taking care not to place too much stuffing in each square as it will be difficult to hold the edges together while sewing. Place open edges of one row of pillows butted to the stitched edge of the next row. Stitch together, using zigzag stitch or similar stitching. Continue joining rows in this way until desired quilt size is reached.

**4** Knot the ends of 25 cm lengths of rouleaux or ribbon and stitch the centre of each length securely to the points where the pillows meet. Tie rouleaux or ribbon into bows.

# Sheets

*These pretty sheets are trimmed with gingham and have a stencilled pattern to match the one on the curtains.*

## MATERIALS

**For each sheet:**
- ☐ 90 cm of 115 cm wide fabric
- ☐ an additional strip, of either contrast or of main fabric, 90 cm x 15 cm for the trimmed band
- ☐ 90 cm x 5 cm strip of gingham fabric
- ☐ matching sewing thread
- ☐ stencilling equipment as for the nursery curtains

## METHOD

1 cm seams allowed throughout.

**1** Mark the positions for the stencilled lambs across the 15 cm wide band. Stencil the band following the stencilling instructions on page 101.

**2** Press under 1 cm on the lower edge of the stencilled band. Place the stencilled band on the top of the sheet so the right side of the band faces the wrong side of the sheet, having the lamb's feet closest to the edge to be stitched. Stitch along the top and side edges of the band and sheet. Turn the band to the right side. Press.

**3** Fold fabric strip over double with wrong sides facing and pin under the pressed edge of the band. Stitch down through all thicknesses. Hem all remaining edges of the sheet to finish. Press.

# Pillow shape

## MATERIALS

- ☐ 30 cm of 115 cm wide fabric to match the sheets
- ☐ a piece of quilter's polyester wadding the size of your pillow shape (see below)
- ☐ sewing thread

## METHOD

1 cm seams allowed throughout.

**1** Make a pattern for pillow shape by tracing the curved outline of the top of your bassinet mattress and have it measure about 30 cm long. It will look a little like a half-circle. Cut two pillow shapes from the main fabric and one from the wadding.

**2** Stencil a lamb on one fabric piece, using the same method as for the sheet band and curtain tie back.

**3** Place wadding against wrong side of the stencilled fabric. Baste together.

**4** Place remaining piece over trimmed piece, right sides facing and raw edges matching. Stitch around edge, with an opening for turning at one side. Turn shape to right side. Press. Hand sew closed.

## PULL OUT PATTERN SHEET GUIDE

The Pull Out Pattern Sheet at the back of the book has the following information:
- ❏ Window measurement diagram for curtains
- ❏ Café Curtain cut-out template
- ❏ Cord threading diagram for the festoon blind
- ❏ Construction diagram for the roman blind
- ❏ Pattern for the director's chair
- ❏ Place mat and napkin embroidery designs
- ❏ Stencils for the quilt, floorcloth and bedhead
- ❏ Bed linen fabric quantities chart
- ❏ Lamb stencils for baby's room

# Down to DETAIL

## Fabric Shelves

*These fabric shelves are ideal storage for a room where floor space is at a premium. You can store a wide variety of things, such as toys, hats or bags and, by adjusting the size of the shelves, you can store much more.*

### MATERIALS

- ☐ 2 m of 115 cm wide large check print fabric
- ☐ 2.20 m of 115 cm wide stripe print fabric
- ☐ 1.50 m of 115 cm wide small check print fabric
- ☐ 5 rectangles of hardboard, each 39 cm x 29 cm

### METHOD

1 cm seams allowed throughout

**1** Cut two rectangles of the large check print fabric for the outside panels, each 152 cm x 32 cm. Cut two rectangles of stripe print fabric for the shelves and back, each 212 cm x 42 cm. Cut eight squares of small check print for the inside panels, each 32 cm x 32 cm, and one rectangle of small check print for the inside top, 62 cm x 32 cm.

**2** With right sides facing, stitch stripe print pieces together along the short edges to form one long strip. Press the seam open. Press under 1 cm at remaining short edges, topstitch and edgestitch to finish.

**3** Fold strip every 30 cm to form five double-thickness open-backed shelves, with four single-thickness backs in between. Press.

**4** With right sides facing, pin one small check print square to the top, back and lower edges of one shelf side. 1 cm seam allowance at front edge of square will extend past finished shelf front. Clipping into corners, stitch around top, back and lower edges to form the shelf side. Press. Repeat for other seven squares to form the entire shelf unit.

**5** With right sides facing, pin one large check print piece to side of shelf unit around front, back and lower edges. Large check print piece will extend 31 cm above top of shelf unit to form top hanging section. Clipping into corners, stitch around front, back and lower edges to enclose all seam allowances. Trim seams and turn to right side. Press. Repeat for the other side.

**6** With right sides facing, stitch top edges of large check print pieces together to form top hanging section. Press seam open.

**7** With right sides facing, stitch small check print rectangle to top hanging section along front edge. Clipping into corners, stitch side edges of rectangle to side edges of top shelf, enclosing all seam allowances. Trim seams, turn to right side. Press.

**8** Press under 1 cm along back edges of top hanging section to enclose remaining seam allowances. Slipstitch together to finish.

**9** Insert five rectangles of hardboard into open backs of shelves to complete shelf unit. Top hanging section should then be suspended from an appropriate wall bracket.

*Above: Fabric shelves*

109

# Index

Laura Ashley (Australia) Pty Limited

# Acknowledgments

The publishers would like to thank the following for their contribution:
Photographs supplied by: Laura Ashley (Australia) Pty Limited; Nairn Floors; Country Form; IKEA; Australian Wool Corporation; Dupont; Lifestyle; Forbo; Amber Tiles
**Jennifer Bennell** for painted finishes
**Bernina** and **Pfaff** for sewing machines
**Boyac, NSW** for braids and tiebacks
**Canning Vale** for towels
**Country Floors, NSW** for pottery accessories
**Curtrax, NSW** for curtain accessories
**Pel Fesq** for leadlight porthole project
**John Kaldor** for furnishing fabrics
**Laura Ashley** for Anaglypta wallpaper and fabrics
**Liberty** for kitchen fabrics
**McCall's** for cushion braid and trims
**Dieter Mylius** for wine rack project
**Offray** for ribbons
**Pebeo** for ceramic paints
**Ray Toby Pty Ltd** for craft fabrics
**Colin Try** for vinyl tile floor and plate rack projects
**Sue and Paul Whitter** for various collections